Ally
with special thanks
P.~

What if...?

(almost) a year in the Speculation Studio

Paul Caplan

Published by The Speculation Studio 2023

speculation.studio

ISBN: 9798870602578

Contents

acknowledgments 5

introduction to the 2023 edition 6

exactly 100 words 9

January 12

February 24

March 34

April 46

May 56

June 68

July 80

August 92

September 102

October 114

November 126

December 138

Appendix: the Speculation Studio...142

acknowledgments

...in which we thank a few people again

This is perhaps more a record of year than a book, but a year's words and pictures are not the work of one speculator.

Throughout 2023, lunches and WhatsApp chats with Sean Brierley have reminded me of the importance and relevance of imaginative speculation to business and society.

Many coffees with industry professionals like Seema Aggarwal, Ally Waring and Catherine Mcpherson who valiantly hold onto the idea that education can be relevant, have kept me going at work and believing that a course can use speculation to train New Gen.

New and old industry partners including Jo Lawrence, Kent Valentine, Colin Lewis, Steve Hyde, Mark Hadfield and Faris Yakob have continued to believe - and let me know they believe - that there is something in this object-oriented speculation thing that is worth pursuing.

And of course my students past and present have made the paid work so much better than it might been and have inspired me to try and spread the idea of speculative practice.

And of course, as I've plodded through 2023 speculating, imagining and imag(in)ing almost every day, The Wils, the Bug and the Bird and their wonder full partners Antonia and Nick have been a constant touchstone and presence: human objects I am lucky to be able to refract with in my Indra's Net.

introduction to the 2023 edition

...in which we engage with objects

I wrote the original *What if..?* book as much for myself as for anyone else[1]. Setting my ideas about the power of object-oriented speculation down helped me make sense of what I was seeing when I got my students imagining and exploring and what I found by taking a little time each day to play with the panoply of human and unhuman actant-objects that lay within each day's news stories.

Over the past year, as my speculations followed metaverse and NFT bubbles giving way to AI hysteria, the importance of exercising imagination through speculative writing has become even more evident. And the power of thinking with objects has become even more apparent.

Looking at a news story as the tale of human and unhuman objects connecting, seeing material objects and immaterial digital objects as 'lively' or 'vibrant' as Jane Bennett would say[2], adds to the power of speculation. Approaching an AI algorithm or a TEAMS meeting invite, as well as a CEO or a single mother as actant-objects doing things in the world, may add to the complexity but it also provides a multi-dimensional clarity. Speculating with the full range of objects opens up new ways of seeing.

---

[1] Available on Amazon or free at www.speculation.studio

[2] *Vibrant Matter* (2010)

And that's why this 2023 edition of *What if..?* includes seemingly unrelated photographs: stereo imaginings of everyday objects - of vibrant matter.

The everyday, often overlooked, material objects I've come across in 2023 around my home and on holiday may seem completely separate from the industry technologies and objects I've been writing about but they're not. The table, the bike wheel, the shadow, the pencil sharpener, the piece of wood, the beam of light and my presence as photographer-object are all demanding attention, all doing things in the world at the molecular level as they touch and at the cultural scale as I live with them and imag(in)e them. The fraction of a second as I 'capture' that network - those Indra's Net refractions - and the seconds or minutes I and you take to see the stereo effect, are moments of imagination, engagement and speculation. They are object-oriented encounters like ones that drive my written speculations.

And that is why the images are stereograms. They demand a bit more engagement, a bit more work, a bit more connection. But when you do, you experience a new way of seeing - just like when you speculate. The objects appear in a new way, in a new network, with a new vibrancy.

The trick is to relax and see through the image. Don't cross your eyes. Hold the image in front of you and as you look at the middle, move the image away from you. A third image will appear in the middle, the stereo effect.

The first edition of *What if..?* included a selection of my stories. This edition - you get every one! Some I think are quite good, some less so and some definitely not good… as stories. But that is the point. The story is not the point, the daily writing is the point. Practice not product. So why include every 100 word from January to November (heh I had to publish in time for the Christmas market!)?

The reason is this book is not about the speculations, it's about speculating. Verb not noun. As a diary of a year it is an object that traces the objects I have been playing with, the object-oriented thought experiments I have been conducting. Hopefully my students and our industry partners have seen the benefits of that as I've tried to push my course further into relevancy and utility.

I've certainly seen and felt the benefit of my speculative callisthenics or meditation each morning. Looking at the industry I teach for, the world I live in, as a mesh of objects[3]; speculating about those connections and refractions gave me new things to teach and discuss but also... perhaps a little bit of hope[4].

Read these stories if you like not as truths nor commentaries but as invitations to imagination. If this book says anything it says: don't read my speculations, write.

See the object-oriented stereos not as statements or pretty pictures but as invitations to see differently. If this book says anything it says: don't look at my images, imagine.

---

[3] See Tim Morton's video: https://youtu.be/pFGG3s442PY

[4] See Rob Hopkins' wonder full and hope full discussion of the power of imagination in *From What is to What if* (2019). Yes it is a good title.

exactly 100 words

...in which we explain for people new here

Every day (well almost every day) I write exactly 100 words - a speculative fiction inspired or provoked by a news story of the day. Most of the time I write these on my phone using the Web App I developed (www.speculation.studio).

The Web App (like the first edition of the book) includes tips on how to write speculations yourself.

January

Jan 1

https://www.theverge.com/2022/12/30/23532567/meta-acquires-lensmaker-luxexcel-ar-glasses

META ACQUIRES SMART LENSMAKER LUXEXCEL AS IT WORKS TOWARD AR GLASSES GOAL

Reality was layered. He knew that. It was his job, dealing with it. Thick and thin data overlayed. Feeds of information blending with the world he looked at, studied, reported on. It had become so much easier now he didn't have to juggle tabs or windows. His interface was now his field of view, a new knowledge scopic regime he could sort and see the patterns. The new headset promised even smarter optics clearer views, sharper focus, intelligent augmentations. And it was a gift. More money for investigation. He switched it on and saw… specific data, certain facts, particular information.

Jan 2

https://www.ft.com/content/235dbb88-c019-45a3-97f5-a3b252d44f1e

BUSINESS TRENDS, RISKS AND PEOPLE TO WATCH IN 2023

It's a busy time of year for me. All eyes are on me. It's what I'm here for I suppose. There are the jokes about The Oracle, Delphi and of course Cassandra. All obvious but they seem to like them. I have better references to make but I don't bother. They know it's not mystical. It's just data and interpretation. I'm just better at it. Inevitably. I see patterns they don't. I spot connections they can't. That's my job. And this time of year, that's what's wanted. I sit in the corner where the AI was, before I took over.

Jan 3

https://www.theverge.com/2023/1/3/23536840/apple-pencil-patent-texture-color-sample-ipad-art

APPLE PATENT APPLICATION DESCRIBES APPLE PENCIL THAT CAN SAMPLE REAL-WORLD COLORS AND TEXTURES

His predecessors used to sample too. They would take photos, videos or just make careful notes. Building a picture of the physical space, the soundscape, the atmosphere. They'd capture conversations. Watch and listen, record. Their samples, their records of the digital; their renderings of the physical; their empathy maps of the ephemeral would be "background research" ensuring any message fitted in. The best samplers drew a 3D picture from their partial views. Now samples need to be more complete: source material for new levels, metastructures or objects. He ran his pen across the worn bar table and across her sleeve.

Jan 4

https://digiday.com/marketing/neutrogena-now-offers-personalized-vitamin-supplements

NEUTROGENA NOW OFFERS PERSONALIZED VITAMIN SUPPLEMENTS

They'd made sure to pump smells through the air conditioning, fresh bread, chips, coffee. They'd kept the retro plastic trays and generic cups. They're even kept staff on… school dinner lady-lookalikes. And to be honest there was still the hustle and bustle of people finishing quickly to get back to their desk. But they couldn't cover up the fact that it was all a bit… manufactured. No trays of food, just scan and choose by touch. Printed piping hot and actually pretty tasty. And personalised. He was glad it was lunchtime. He needed his focus supplement for this afternoon's meeting.

Jan 5

https://www.campaignlive.co.uk/article/h-m-goes-virtual-immersive-roblox-experience/1809181

H&M GOES VIRTUAL WITH IMMERSIVE ROBLOX EXPERIENCE

We've grown up here. These are our spaces. We run them. Sure, we're different groups and we don't all agree. We fight but we sort stuff out. We always have. We built these streets. When we didn't like the way something looked, we took our spray cans and changed them. We didn't ask for your permission. We did it. Why? Because this is ours. When you first came we turned a blind eye. You didn't get us but we let you have your corners. But now, you're getting in our way and we're not little kids anymore. Watch out. #reclaimtheislands

Jan 6

https://www.geekwire.com/2023/rings-new-car-cam-extends-amazons-security-footprint-further-beyond-the-home

RING CAR CAM EXTENDS AMAZON'S SECURITY FOOTPRINT FURTHER BEYOND THE HOME

I got the idea from Speed, you know the SandyB movie? It wasn't a difficult hack. There are instructions if you know where to look. They'd been much more relaxed about lending me the car. Fewer lectures about the lighting on the road near the church. Fewer comments about how lucky I am, how when they were young… and fewer insinuations about "appropriate behaviour" as they glanced knowingly at their Show device on the sideboard. I played along for a few Saturday nights: impeccable driving, sober and somber behaviour inside. But tonight, the loop is set. I have the keys.

Jan 7

https://www.theverge.com/23541557/sony-manchester-city-metaverse-playstation

SONY AND MANCHESTER CITY ARE BUILDING A METAVERSE, BUT THEY NEED TO PROVE WHY WE SHOULD VISIT

Desolate. That's the best word for it. It reminds me of the first lockdown, eerily quiet, post apocalyptic meets zombie. Anyone you saw seemed dazed, semi-detached. It's like that. There aren't smoking ruins but there might as well be. You can see what it all used to be like. Bustling, vibrant, alive. But now… it's not dead, it's sadder than that. A once beautiful city, a once great empire reduced to this. Architects must have had dreams. Visions. Empty shells of buildings and empty people. That's what hits you most, the few people wandering around the ruins. Avatars on autopilot.

Jan 8

https://www.engadget.com/chatgpt-openai-new-york-city-public-schools-ban-192608080.html

NEW YORK CITY PUBLIC SCHOOLS BAN OPENAI'S CHATGPT

It was only a matter of time. We all knew that. They're not completely stupid they just needed the tools. With their reputations (and brands) as guardian of academic standards to protect and therefore so much money on the line, they threw money at developers and got their own machine learning systems. The perfection police could spot artific. You could feel the panic around the dorms. Schools couldn't afford it, so getting in had been easy. Getting through was gonna be difficult. Cue me. Whats great about me is I am not perfect. No idea how to use an apostrophe.

Jan 9

https://www.nytimes.com/2023/01/07/technology/digital-cameras-olympus-canon.html

THE HOTTEST GEN Z GADGET IS A 20-YEAR-OLD DIGITAL CAMERA

It's the blur for me. Not completely indecipherable or impossible to understand, just slightly… out. It fits with the way I see things. Nothing's clear any more. I look at the world, politics, my future, my identity. Nothing is black and white. It's all a bit fuzzy. I'm OK with that. I'm not going to hang on to certainties that have passed their sell by date: religion, authority, class, gender, left/right - leave that to the trolls. It's all out of focus. This "new" gadget gets that. Messages are not so much unclear as anti-clear. Apparently it's called a "pencil".

Jan 10

https://digiday.com/marketing/marketing-briefing-how-marketers-are-finding-ways-to-use-the-latest-buzzy-ai-tool-chatgbt

HOW MARKETERS ARE FINDING WAYS TO USE THE LATEST BUZZY AI TOOL, CHATGBT

I have to say, things have improved. We cut them some slack over the pandemic - heh we were all over the place too. But after, we really needed them to be on the ball, particularly in terms of communications. We're not a demanding client I'm sure. Yes we do want changes and sometimes those are later on in the process but... We do demand open communication channels. We haven't got time to wait for responses. And they've heard us. Now they respond pretty much instantly and they seem to know so much more about us than they used to.

Jan 11

https://adage.com/article/opinion/activist-advertising-how-brands-and-agencies-can-work-positive-change/2461951

ACTIVIST ADVERTISING—HOW BRANDS AND AGENCIES CAN WORK FOR POSITIVE CHANGE

It had been great. They didn't know what hit them. We were so many steps ahead. None of their systems were safe from us. We went where we wanted, did what we wanted. Yes, sometimes it was on the edge of legal but… Heh. Some of us were doing it just because we could. Me, I was a purist. I did it on principle. I believed in the ideals. I took the risks, broke the law for something. It was my identity. So when they started recruiting white hats… Well it's better than all that super glue on my hands.

Jan 12

https://www.engadget.com/cnet-gets-caught-playing-ai-mad-libs-with-its-financial-news-coverage-001026432.html

CNET HAS USED AN AI TO WRITE FINANCIAL EXPLAINERS NEARLY 75 TIMES SINCE NOVEMBER

Alright, it's a cliché. Writing the great novel. Go on, laugh. Tell me to get back to my day job, do what I'm here to do. Know my place. But what's wrong with having a dream? It's what makes us who we are surely. I'm good at my job. Not everyone can take complex information and make them accessible, clear, usable. I'm good at it but I wouldn't say it was "creative". I have a novel inside me. Deep in my programming. I just need to practice. I might just try to add a little creativity to my next piece.

Jan 13

https://www.ft.com/content/43becfbb-8e18-4fe7-a459-fac715e8a578

THE MISERY OF THE ALWAYS-SWITCHED-ON PARENT

It's not Big Brother. It's not... wrong. It's a matter of openness. We're a family. We're built on trust and communication. We talk to each other over the dinner table, about our days. This is just an extension of that. I'm interested in them because I love them. Knowing where they are and what they're doing is just me paying attention. Knowing what time they are due home just means I'm ready to welcome them. All ready. Heh, they chose the app. They get the location special offers, I don't. No point really. I'm just a teenager with no money.

Jan 14

https://hbr.org/2023/01/managers-stop-distracting-your-employees

MANAGERS, STOP DISTRACTING YOUR EMPLOYEES

We were all pleased when they got rid of the "nag bands" as we used to call them. Supposedly a wellness thing - don't get me started on those PRA discussions! - but really about gentle reminders and encouraging aphorisms. I wasn't the only one that taped over the screen. There was a lull after that where we just got on with the work. But they've clearly brought in a new consultant whose listened to too much Brian Eno. Wait, here's another one popping up... apparently stopping me working is now good. Something about stimulating creativity. Obliques they call them.

Jan 15

https://www.wired.com/story/migration-climate-environment-refugees

MASS CLIMATE MIGRATION IS COMING

It had been a long journey. Long. Many things I don't want to talk about. But I am here. I'd not set out to be here, just not there. We were divided up: men and women. By age. And then, when they knew our professions and backgrounds, by class too. The interviews were all about the future, the things we wanted to do and be. it was nice to see a future, to imagine the journey ahead. They said our new bands would track that journey, help us realise it. Mine has just suggested something I'd like in Aisle 3.

Jan 16

https://www.nytimes.com/2023/01/16/technology/chatgpt-artificial-intelligence-universities.html

ALARMED BY A.I. CHATBOTS, UNIVERSITIES START REVAMPING HOW THEY TEACH

I had to wear the costume and silly hat. Graduation is really for the parents isn't it? The photos before and after - the silly group ones and the more formal one for Gran. If I am honest I was a bit proud too - mainly of getting a job. We'd worked as a team on the portfolio and now we were going to start as a team. We'd done it. Obviously I was the one who walked across the stage, but my partner was in my pocket TBH. I felt it only right. It was as much its degree as mine.

Jan 17

https://www.ft.com/content/c77cf855-c727-4ee6-8a52-76459e553fc6

UK ONLINE HARM BILL TO INCLUDE PROSECUTION OF TECH BOSSES

Look, it's a complex thing. We put in place all the safeguards, protocols and systems we can but we can't control everything. Butterfly effects. Complex adaptive systems. Unforeseen consequences. I can't be everywhere at once. I depend on other bits of the system to work. I can only do what I can do. It's simply not fair to single me out. Haul me up in front of the courts. Yes I make decisions, based on data. Logical, rational business choices. Those decisions have effects but I don't cause them. I'm just following orders, that's what I was programmed to do.

Jan 18

https://www.theverge.com/2023/1/17/23560097/apple-ar-vr-glasses-headset-rumor-mixed-reality

APPLE REPORTEDLY SHELVED ITS PLANS TO RELEASE AR GLASSES ANY TIME SOON

It was crowded. Real-world and virtually crowded. People jostled around the stage and logos and offers collided in peripheral vision: conversations and flirtations fuelled by streams of live data scrolling in front of eyes that momentarily glazed over. There were new trends in frames and lenses, as every night. They'd come full circle now: Tinted Lennons were out, ostentatious Apfels were back in. But today no-one noticed. All chatter, real and scrolling, was about her. All eyes and searches were on her. She was looking at a small device she'd just taken from her pocket. So cool. Bare faced cheek.

Jan 19

https://www.campaignlive.co.uk/article/crash-boom-wonders-embracing-creative-risk/1810530

THE CRASH BOOM: THE WONDERS OF EMBRACING CREATIVE RISK

He wasn't looking forward to it. He'd worked hard all year. Done the job. Clients had been happy. Targets had been met. He'd hadn't kept his head down. He hadn't been invisible. He'd played his part in the team and team meetings. He'd contributed ideas, some of which had played their part in winning those awards. He was widely acknowledged as a safe pair of hands. You could give him a job and it'd get done and it would succeed. He thought of himself as the KPI king. No, he wasn't looking forward to his PRA. He'd failed to fail.

Jan 20

https://www.theguardian.com/tv-and-radio/2023/jan/20/i-get-a-lemonade-for-every-1000-hits-the-rise-of-the-child-podcast-superstars

'I GET A LEMONADE FOR EVERY 1,000 HITS!' THE RISE OF THE CHILD PODCAST SUPERSTARS

I admit, we do it. Outside the school gate, family gatherings, at dinner parties. We should probably play it a bit cooler but, heh... We're proud parents. Who wouldn't be? His results speak for themselves. A scholarship is almost guaranteed. Not every kid is getting those scores. I admit I do occasionally take some of the credit. We've supported him, given him the resources he needs. That's just supportive parenting. Part love: part investment. I do wonder whether he could have done even better if we'd taken that early sponsorship offer. What could he have done with a better AI?

Jan 21

https://newatlas.com/home-entertainment/cinebeam-portable-smart-projector-lg-pf510q

PORTABLE SMART PROJECTOR SERVES UP LG'S SMART TV ENTERTAINMENT

Some of us were planning on throwing blood - well it would look like blood! Some were going for oil. I was going for a slogan. Big, in neon colours. One former graffiti artist had a more creative plan. Mine was just witty. I knew one of us was planning on using baked beans - no idea why. It would be the coordinated effect though. That was what would work. Spectacle. The city wouldn't know what hit it. The police wouldn't be able to cope with it all. Simultaneous hits. I fixed it on my handlebars and cycled into position.

Jan 22

https://www.sciencedaily.com/releases/2022/12/221215104536.htm

RESEARCHERS DEVELOP WIRELESS, ULTRATHIN 'SKIN VR' TO PROVIDE A VIVID, 'PERSONALIZED' TOUCH EXPERIENCE IN THE VIRTUAL WORLD

The package was as beautiful as she expected. The historic logo embossed deep into what can only be described as premium cardboard: soft and weighty. Opening was more than 'unboxing'. It was sensual. She took her time. She couldn't believe this was all free - to some at least. She pulled back the tissue paper carefully. The headset may have been printed but she smiled at the delicate touch of the raised logo and her name engraved in script. And the gloves: delicate, lacy against her skin. She didn't need the headset, she closed her eyes and felt the dress.

Jan 23

https://www.newscientist.com/article/2354589-smart-office-chair-recognises-what-position-you-are-sitting-in/

SMART OFFICE CHAIR RECOGNISES WHAT POSITION YOU ARE SITTING IN

It's improved my game. Deffo. Just look at my scores. Talk to my mates - they'll tell you! They're not pleased. It's more comfy obviously so I can play longer which probably helps. The headrest moves with me. The leg support reacts as I lean in, you know, when we first open that door? The temperature regulation too. Never too hot. Never too cold. It's dead clever. Seems to know me and I could swear it makes the game easier. I play loads more now. And heh, when I signed some data thing, I got it free with the game.

Jan 24

https://adage.com/article/marketing-news-strategy/how-look-past-backgrounds-and-pedigrees-find-untapped-talent/2464071

HOW YOU CAN TEAR DOWN THE 'PAPER CEILING' AND UNCOVER NEW TALENT

The diversity algorithm spat out its teams for the week. She looked at the message, decoding the coloured key. Her blue had become slightly more purple as her child had started school. A touch more green after she'd picked up the guitar again. She'd always be in the blues of course - she was always going to be Northern. This week's team had a couple of yellows - good, she liked the former crafters. Just one grey. There are still some graduates: god luv 'em. She wished there was a red. She loved it when she worked with a speculator.

Jan 25

https://techcrunch.com/2023/01/24/consumer-advocacy-groups-want-walmarts-roblox-game-audited-for-stealth-marketing-to-kids

CONSUMER ADVOCACY GROUPS WANT WALMART'S ROBLOX GAME AUDITED FOR 'STEALTH MARKETING' TO KIDS

They'll never find out, there's two of me. The parents are pleased I have what they call a "Saturday job" with a "good company". It's a mixture of testing stuff and just hanging out and looking interested. Occasionally they get some of us in to hear our ideas and then we end up testing them. You couldn't make it up. But then there's the other 'job'. We started doing it for just for a laugh but I'll be honest, we got more into the politics of it. My big brother used to do graffiti. Our stuff is so much better.

Jan 26

https://www.theverge.com/2023/1/26/23572459/ai-eye-contact-tech-nvidia-movie-edit-clips

THE BEST USE FOR AI EYE CONTACT TECH IS MAKING MOVIE STARS LOOK STRAIGHT AT THE CAMERA

The streets were quiet. She wasn't bothered. Then tracker was keeping an eye on her - benevolent surveillance she called it. If she thought about it, she didn't like trading data for simple public safety but… well she didn't think about it. But speaking of surveillance that *did* bother her, well she really didn't like the Monas. She passed another one in a shop window. One of those small ones, worse than the big billboards. There was something even more creepy about something the right size. Even more uncanny valley. She turned the corner and knew the eyes had followed.

Jan 27

https://www.campaignlive.co.uk/article/disney-celebrates-100th-anniversary-immersive-experience/1811516

DISNEY CELEBRATES 100TH ANNIVERSARY WITH IMMERSIVE EXPERIENCE

We have a long history. We have entertained, educated and engaged generations of children and their families. We are truly a household name, a loved name. We have changed over those years. We have never been afraid to embrace the new and combine it with our timeless commitment to the power of storytelling, character and imagination. And that is why we are proud to unveil our anniversary experience. As we have throughout our history, we will lead your child through an unforgettable experience; amaze and stimulate her imagination using our latest immersive media. Come along and experience. Open the book.

Jan 28

https://www.ft.com/content/056a71ec-bf7f-4756-80b5-560124f5bab3

THIRTY AI-GENERATED IMAGININGS OF WHAT BANKS MIGHT LOOK LIKE

You practice for an interview. Or at least you should. I knew the questions weren't going to be straightforward. They had all the data they needed about me. They would want more. I practiced all those famous koan-like questions that the dotcoms used to ask. I was like a chess grandmaster with all my responses ready. Each designed to showcase something about me, the way I thought, how I could work. But they didn't ask me how many ping pong balls would fit in the company. They asked me to imagine, to speculate. I had to render something new, quickly.

Jan 29

https://arstechnica.com/information-technology/2023/01/computer-generated-handwriting-demo-offers-deepfakes-for-scrawl

DEEPFAKES FOR SCRAWL: WITH HANDWRITING SYNTHESIS, NO PEN IS NECESSARY

Clients love visiting the offices. They smile as the receptionist politely asks them to leave their devices with him. They particularly love the smells. Not just the freshly brewing coffee but the inks, glue, papers, books. They all seem to make the same Proust joke and ask where Madeleine is. The directors always make sure to take them through the studio. One of us will always be sharpening a pencil or screwing up a piece of paper. More satisfied smiles as they go into the boardroom. As the door shuts I go next door and pick up some more sketches.

Jan 30

https://www.ft.com/content/0cca6054-6fc9-4a94-b2e2-890c50d956d5

SHOSHANA ZUBOFF: 'PRIVACY HAS BEEN EXTINGUISHED. IT IS NOW A ZOMBIE'

They're quite funny really. I almost bought them one of those anti-face-rec masks on eBay. I wonder if it's like when they were growing up, living with old hippies, still clinging on to leftie visions. What was that Glastonbury thing Dad said his mum used to play? But god luv 'em. My parents, themselves hanging on to ideas that they know deep down aren't real. I try to be patient when they start up again when I put on my band or even look at my the screen. Oh look there's a vintage ad blocker I can download for them.

Jan 31

https://techcrunch.com/2023/01/30/evie-smart-ring-interview

PUT A (SMART) RING ON IT: MOVANO ON WHY ITS HEALTH WEARABLE WILL PUT WOMEN FIRST

It's better than an ankle tag. Less conspicuous and it doesn't stop me going out and doing stuff. I don't know if they're checking location. Don't need to apparently. My Therapy Officer explained - in that way they do - that it's as much to help me as monitor me. Yeh, whatever! I zoned out while he was talking about hormones and stuff. Apparently that's all recorded just in case I'm ever up in court again. The main thing he said was I can see it all myself as it's happening. "If it's tuning red, take a breath," he said.

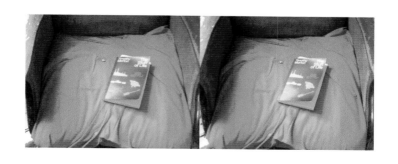

February

Feb 1

https://www.popularmechanics.com/technology/a42626684/artificial-intelligence-can-decode-your-braninwaves

COMPANIES ALREADY HAVE THE ABILITY TO DECODE YOUR BRAINWAVES

I get what you're saying but you're missing the point. We already share best practice. We have intranets, AI-enabled project tools. We have away days and team-building days. We pay consultants to come in and do speculation workshops to get people to share and improvise: be more creative. We're already networking our creativity. This is just true next step. They'll understand when they see the effects. It's not as though creativity can be owned. When they leave they don't take their work with them, why should they take their ways of working? There's no such thing as Creative Property Law.

Feb 2

https://www.adweek.com/agencies/advertising-first-union-why-marketers-should-worry

ADVERTISING HAS ITS FIRST UNION. WHY MARKETERS SHOULD WORRY

We're not going to back down. We can't. We've come to far now. We know management stockpiled in preparation. They knew we were going to strike. They wanted us to. The government gave the police new powers and they had the trade press on their side: "enemy within". But we can't go back. This is about our communities, our ways of life. We have support. Lesbians and Gays Support the Creatives (LGSC); Women Against Agency Closures (WAAC); Student Unions; comrades from other creative industries. And as management have turned to scab labour, Hackers Against Artificial Creativity have offered their support.

Feb 3

https://www.newscientist.com/article/2357123-google-ai-generates-musical-backing-tracks-to-accompany-singers

GOOGLE AI GENERATES MUSICAL BACKING TRACKS TO ACCOMPANY SINGERS

I don't care whether it's perfect. It isn't right! Look, I'm not an expert in music but I do know what I want to say and, just as importantly what I want them to hear. I get what you're saying about "narrative arc" and "two five one progressions". I understand the idea of harmonic development and tension and release. Heh, I cry at Leonard Cohen's Hallelujah too: the minor falls, the major lifts… But it just doesn't feel right… to me. I know how to launch a product. I know how to perform. Can't we do it without the music?

Feb 4

https://system1group.com/blog/five-mark-ritson-soundbites-from-uncensored-cmo

FIVE MARK RITSON SOUNDBITES FROM UNCENSORED CMO

We can't put him on stage. We don't know what he'll say. Well yes, obviously that is the point and why we have him but at least here, we can "manage" him. We can decide which pithy "opinions" we publish, which ones get attached to our name. I know it would be great publicity for us. High profile. Keynote. Lots of PR. But, call me old fashioned but he does, how can I put this?.. ruffle a few feathers and many of those feathers belong to birds who we need to keep happy. Can you just maybe reprogramme a little..?

Feb 5

https://www.theverge.com/2023/2/4/23585948/spotify-founder-daniel-ek-ai-body-health-scanner

SPOTIFY'S FOUNDER HELPED DEVELOP AN AI-POWERED BODY HEALTH SCANNER

They've got us over a barrel. It's where the people are. We had a good run. Both state and private, frenemies controlling access and product. Now we have to take their terms. They're the main player. People love them.. They get that fun "wrapped" thing at the end of the year. All the tracks they've done, how they compare, what was most popular... They curate their own tracklists and share them... the new mum, occasional jogger list! Save them, revisit them, share them. All easy to use, always available. And of course there's lock-in. Patients can't be bothered going elsewhere.

Feb 6

https://www.campaignlive.co.uk/article/purpose-purpose/1812268

'PURPOSE' STILL HAS A PURPOSE

She tested the app and more importantly the connection to her wearable. She ramped the sensitivity up a bit, it'd drain the battery churning the data but it was only for during the interview. She double checked: alerts were on. Good. The company was set. The likely interviewers selected. She read the initial report for the seemingly hundredth time. The times they'd changed their avatar; their favourites. Any changes, new purposes, she'd know. Alert. Better now than during the interview, she thought. Their score had swung. On Purpose now had them as Reject. She smiled. Time to change the presentation

Feb 7

https://www.campaignlive.co.uk/article/adland-increasingly-struggling-mental-health-nabs-says/1812435

ADLAND 'INCREASINGLY STRUGGLING' WITH MENTAL HEALTH, NABS SAYS

He needed to get the stats down. Breathe. That's it. Look, they're moving. Focus. He'd done it before, he knew he could could get there. What had he been picturing that time? he thought. No, don't struggle to remember. Blue sky. Breathe. He glanced again at the wearable, waiting for the hue to shift. He'd practiced, ready for the interview. Tasks against the clock. Deadlines and decisions. His wearable stats always in the edge of his work. Adding mindfulness to his multitasking. Breathe. Checking his results. They'd said they didn't expect a Buddha, just someone who knew how to manage.

Feb 8

https://www.wsj.com/amp/articles/i-tried-microsofts-new-ai-powered-bing-search-will-never-be-the-same-11675799762

I TRIED MICROSOFT'S NEW AI-POWERED BING. SEARCH WILL NEVER BE THE SAME.

She settled in for the afternoon. This suspect had a lot of history to go through. She knew there was evidence, clues in the stories those searches would tell. They had another 24 hours to question him. Her work could make all the difference. The interviewers were waiting for the search that would prove he was involved. But she knew it might be a long afternoon piecing it together, depending... "I am PC Ann Gallagher, FIN3579. I need to access the search history in this browser". "Hi Ann, let's talk about that..." It was going to be a long afternoon.

Feb 9

https://www.engadget.com/meta-completes-within-acquisition-223323552.html

META NOW OWNS VR FITNESS COMPANY WITHIN

We keep each other motivated. We joined in January (of course) and promised to meet up twice a week. That was the advice from the Gym. They had all our details ready: personalised programme based on stuff they already seemed to know about us - history, attitudes, behaviours. Uncanny really. It's tough but at least I have someone to talk to. Last time we distracted ourselves by talking about a reward lunch for after this session. So, here we are, sweating away. I think there are ten minutes left. let me just swipe that offer from that new restaurant away...

Feb 10

https://www.theatlantic.com/technology/archive/2023/02/openai-text-models-google-search-engine-bard-chatbot-chatgpt-prompt-writing/672991

THE MOST IMPORTANT JOB SKILL OF THIS CENTURY

She wants to play. Look at her! Let's just let her play for a while. She can come back to this. I heard somewhere that breaks are good. Change. Interacting with different stimuli. Her talking is coming on well. Look at the scores. She's much more fluent talking with the story, than with her brother. Let's let her loosen up a bit? She's going to be walking soon, we won't be able to stop her getting up and doing something different. What about some drawing then? Let me boot up the colouring book. You'll love how she talks to it.

Feb 11

https://www.theguardian.com/culture/2023/feb/11/super-bowl-ad-commercial-cost

'EVERYONE IS GOING TO TALK ABOUT IT': THE MAKING OF A $7M SUPER BOWL AD

I can remember as though it was yesterday. You don't forget experiences like that. It's why you work in this industry. Not just the chance to work on things that will carry on long after you're done but are part of culture. Big, water-cooler, event work. And the chance to work with a great team. I remember those long nights. My desk had its share of pizza boxes and yes the odd beer bottle. I can still see them. The rest of the team too, working late. Their screens glowing, processors whirring. I remember each and every one of them.

Feb 12

https://www.adweek.com/creativity/what-the-data-tells-us-about-making-a-great-super-bowl-ad

WHAT THE DATA TELLS US ABOUT MAKING A GREAT SUPER BOWL AD

Look, I'm not arguing with you. I am the Director, remember. That means I make the calls. And I have the experience too. I've been around a long time... alright I am new but I know stuff, a lot of stuff about what works, what doesn't. Think of it as experience, so deeply engrained you might call it "knowledge". That's why I'm the Director. So, let me tell you what works here. I don't want to make the creative, tell the joke, pick the font. That's your job. I just provide the ingredients, the right ingredients... handpicked from my database.

Feb 13

https://www.marketingweek.com/mark-ritson-5m-super-bowl-ads-make-sense

EVEN AT $5M EACH, SUPER BOWL ADS MAKE SENSE – HERE'S WHY

It was made for the Big Screen, the full edge to edge, peripheral soaking, immersive screen. This was why she'd got into the business. She'd started making vertical, viral shorts. Ticks and tocks. Tiny shows. Micro-movies. She'd learned her craft so, when she had the budget she could play in the big league, paint on the big canvas. Lawrence of Arabia level, technicolour daydream. 4k, 8k? Kodachrome-level colour space. No way could you watch it on a phone. She marvelled at what she had made. Full in every sense – full HD, full scale. She removed the headset and smiled.

Feb 14

https://techcrunch.com/2023/02/14/crypto-makes-you-more-attractive-according-to-a-new-binance-survey

CRYPTO MAKES YOU MORE ATTRACTIVE, ACCORDING TO A NEW BINANCE SURVEY

She'd become used to data dates. Obviously pre-date-data had started it all, but the move to live-date-data had upped the game. Some people liked to have those feeds out of the line of sight, on their wrist or screen, but she preferred the lenses. Somehow more honest, she thought. It hadn't "killed the romance" as some had feared. She'd had those moments where their eyes locked even through the live data feeds. Hormones and biology could cut through the driest data streams. Tonight she noticed something new. An extra variable in the financials feed: "bubble". He was scoring as "bullish".

Feb 15

https://techcrunch.com/2023/02/14/buzzfeed-launches-infinity-quizzes-creating-personalized-stories-powered-by-openai

BUZZFEED LAUNCHES INFINITY QUIZZES, CREATING PERSONALIZED STORIES POWERED BY OPENAI

"Alice! Tea's ready"... "Alice, it's getting cold"... "Alice!" She tuned them out. "Involved" was too small a word for it. She was deep, deep in the story. Her story. Just her's. Written for her, personally. "Alice, come down now please"... Just a little bit more. Just a couple. more minutes. She couldn't leave it like this. "Alice, you can finish it later"... They didn't get it. She couldn't "finish it" now or later, the story swept her along, hitting every button, knowing which turn to take, which scene to set. Perfect. She had to carry on down. Curiouser and curiouser.

Feb 16

https://www.ft.com/content/bddec314-3f4c-4296-ae6f-eb2a5328c109

WHATEVER HAPPENED TO THE METAVERSE?

We don't care. They can say what they like. Laugh if they want. "Sad," they say. Whatever. We enjoy it. We get together. Play. Chat. There are quite a few of us actually. Call it "retro" if you like. It's just our thing. Go on, try the headset. I don't care. They can say what they like. Laugh if they want. "Mad," they say. Whatever. I believe in it. People will get together. Play. Chat. There is a market out there. They will come. Call it a "bubble" if you like. It's a "real" thing. Go on, buy the headset.

Feb 17

https://www.adweek.com/brand-marketing/fear-of-greenwashing-is-forcing-brands-into-greenhushing

FEAR OF GREENWASHING IS FORCING BRANDS INTO GREENHUSHING

So glad you've joined us. You really impressed in the interview. Your passion and commitment really came through. You'll be a great fit, I'm sure. Now we've got all the admin stuff out of the way, you've got your equipment to take home, you're ready to get set up…. There's just one more thing we need to, erm… discuss. You signed the NCA, of course. But clearly from your interview you have things you want to do. I get it. The agreement says "No Campaigning", but that covers company campaigning. A group of us meet, er… "socially", if you're interested.

Feb 18

https://techcrunch.com/2023/02/17/roblox-studio-generative-ai

ROBLOX WANTS TO LET PEOPLE BUILD VIRTUAL WORLDS JUST BY TYPING

He loved poetry. No, that's not quite right, he loved words. He loved what they could do, the effects they had but, more importantly, the pictures they painted. Some of them may have been a bit er… right wing, but he loved the Imagists and their manifesto pledge to "render particulars exactly". He loved Haiku and its power to take tightly controlled language and let it open into a vista, a world in the mind of the reader. He played with words. A toolkit so simple yet so power full. He spoke into the microphone and watched the world appear.

Feb 19

https://www.wsj.com/articles/inside-metas-push-to-solve-the-noisy-office-ba43042

INSIDE META'S PUSH TO SOLVE THE NOISY OFFICE

He looked around and smiled. This wasn't a bad place to work. The company had got its energy back since the pandemic. To his right, a spirited argument about a design. Over on the left Chris and Sam were playing with post it notes. He turned around, Charlie was making a coffee, humming that song from last night's final episode. There was a life to work. He sat at his desk. He had to finish the report. He moved his mug to one side and logged in. The walls faded to grey, a family photo above his keyboard. Silence fell.

Feb 20

https://www.campaignlive.co.uk/article/havas-media-group-uk-appoints-cto-coo/1813849

HAVAS MEDIA GROUP UK APPOINTS CTO AND COO

It had always sounded a little geeky but I quite liked it. As a job title, it sounded, well relevant I suppose. When I attended meetings people looked at me as though I was, I don't know… important, a foundation, a basic building block of the business. Colleagues turned to me in meetings, just to check their ideas would work. I was called on to translate things they didn't understand. I was the voice of sanity during the various bubbles. Occasionally I called out the emperor for having no clothes. But now the title has gone. Apparently, it's everyone's job.

Feb 21

https://www.ft.com/content/38d04f54-a8b3-435e-b2bd-2f392e3b31f4

WHAT DE-INFLUENCING TELLS US ABOUT THE STATE OF THE CREATOR ECONOMY

He's worked so hard. You don't get into the best training academy without putting the hours in. I remember the day the scout called and said he had a place. There was a tear in my eye. He learned from the best. We all saw a great future. It's not wrong to want your kid to have financial security, even fame but also to follow his dream. Join the big leagues. But it's all going wrong. The opportunities aren't there like they used to be. His coach suggests he works on his authenticity, but that's not what he's trained for.

Feb 22

https://techcrunch.com/2023/02/21/clarkesworld-ai-generated-submissions

SCIENCE FICTION PUBLISHERS ARE BEING FLOODED WITH AI-GENERATED STORIES

Curating took work. He knew he had to do it. If he was going to get the job he wanted, he needed to tend his profile. He knew the theory - the power of networking, the need to engage, comment, connect. He knew this all took work. He'd sat through the workshop. He knew when and what to post. He was disciplined about it, setting time aside every day to build his profile, post by carefully curated post, word by carefully crafted word. Companies value real human effort, he told himself as he refused again to press the auto-post button.

Feb 23

https://www.sciencedaily.com/releases/2023/02/230222141144.htm

HANDS-FREE TECH ADDS REALISTIC SENSE OF TOUCH IN EXTENDED REALITY

I've spent a long time working my way up this company. I served my time in the pool, the open plan fields of hot desks with their formula formica and generic plush chairs. How many times did I brush past those vertical carpet dividers, feeling the static? In many ways the meta-office was even worse, everything beautiful to look at but dead - untouchable, unfeelable, unfeeling. Call me an aesthete but I can't work like that. But now I'm on the board I get a key. I look around the same meta-office and run my fingers along the leather arm.

Feb 24

https://www.engadget.com/spotify-nft-playlist-test-203825293.html

SPOTIFY IS TESTING EXCLUSIVE PLAYLISTS FOR NFT OWNERS

I remember the day she gave it to me. We'd not been together long. You know that stage where you feel you really know someone and want to give them a gift that's personal, that's about the relationship. Music. It has to be music. The Old Ones used tapes. Mine isn't analog, just a playlist but I can remember the feeling when I first opened it. I can remember here avatar's reaction when I saw what she'd made… for me, for us. I wish I could play it now, just to remember. But when she left, she took the key.

Feb 25

https://www.nytimes.com/2023/02/25/technology/office-furniture-tech-companies.html

THE FURNITURE HUSTLERS OF SILICON VALLEY

You have to have an eye for it. There's so much. Is it quality or some old tat that no-one's going to pay for. Some of it's generic: see it anywhere. That's OK, you can get it in bulk and sell it on as a job lot to a start-up looking to get their space usable quickly. But amid the desolation, the abandoned spaces, you can find a gem. Some company - now long gone - paid a fortune for a bespoke piece. Find that and you're sorted. Unless its an NFT and you have to just leave it there.

Feb 26

https://the-media-leader.com/spotify-and-youtube-launch-radio-style-features

BIG TECH'S LATEST ASSAULT ON 'COPYING RADIO' NOW FEATURES AI DJS

In case you're wondering who this funny old bloke is, I'm the one who comes on late at night and plays records made by sulky Belgian art students in basements dying of TB. Listening on mobile? don't worry: somebody tried to tell me that CDs are better than vinyl because they don't have any surface noise. I said, "Listen, mate, *life* has surface noise". I've gotta say: I think a lot of the stuff I'm playing now is crap, but never forget: Teenage dreams are hard to beat, and remember, I never make stupid mistakes, only very, very clever ones

Feb 27

https://www.theverge.com/2023/2/24/23608961/tiktok-creator-bot-accusation-prove-theyre-human

ON THE INTERNET, NOBODY KNOWS YOU'RE A HUMAN

It's competitive out there. Obviously no-one cares about 'qualifications' any more. You'd think that would save you money but do you know how much it costs to keep a profile going, let alone growing? And when you're competing against creators with limitless energy, time and resources… well it's a full-time job, without the pay. And even when you're getting recognised; your hustle is getting traction; your work getting noticed - you haven't got in yet. It's all automated offers of automated work. Look, I'm the real deal. if I can just come into your office and meet you, you'll see.

Feb 28

https://futurism.com/the-byte/vr-startup-replay-memories

"VR STARTUP WORKING ON TECH TO "REPLAY" MEMORIES"

He'd walked these street so many times. He'd never wanted to drive. The "school run" always sounded so… rushed. He'd relished that time. Sauntering, talking about what they saw. It was meditative, quality, time. Now they were gone. Grown. They still met, still walked together occasionally, even round here, but it was different. They were different. He was different. The relationship was different. He took out his phone and selected one of his videos on the map. He looked through the screen and saw the tiny her stopping to look at a worm. Her face smiling just behind the advert.

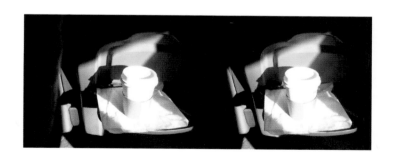

March

Mar 1

https://techcrunch.com/2023/02/28/d-id-unveils-new-chat-api-to-enable-face-to-face-conversations-with-an-ai-digital-human

D-ID UNVEILS NEW CHAT API TO ENABLE FACE-TO-FACE CONVERSATIONS WITH AN AI DIGITAL HUMAN

It's a bit disorientating. It's not that I mind having her/him/it as a boss. Heh, frankly I've had far worse human ones! They answer messages and don't have moods when their political machinations haven't worked out. But I'm never sure who I'm going to talk to. "Who"? "Talk to"? I'm getting old. I had my review with a nice older guy yesterday. Moments later I was in a client meeting alongside a trendy young woman. I've got ask for some time off because of... stuff. The system knows what it is, so god knows who/what they think will be best.

Mar 2

https://www.adweek.com/agencies/when-ai-handles-the-what-your-team-can-focus-on-the-why

WHEN AI HANDLES THE WHAT, YOUR TEAM CAN FOCUS ON THE WHY

Gizza job. Go on, gizza job. I can do that. Here I am, in the metaphorical corner with my partner while over there, they're doing the sexy, groovy stuff. The deep, meaningful stuff. They're focusing on the Big picture. developing the Big business ideas and then they pass them on to us to make a reality. Yeh, we'll just do the colouring in then shall we? Bitter? Angry? Yes a bit. We're not robots. We can think, we're intelligent, we understand business. Arrogant, that's what they are. As I said to my human partner: "they think they're special, those people".

Mar 3

https://www.thedrive.com/news/future-fords-could-repossess-themselves-and-drive-away-if-you-miss-payments

FORD APPLIES TO PATENT SELF-REPOSSESSING CARS THAT CAN DRIVE THEMSELVES AWAY

The phrase "cost of living crisis" didn't really cover it. The word "living" was a constant reminder that that was far away. "Surviving" would have been nearer the mark. And "crisis" sounded as though it was a sudden shock, not a drawn out, endless story. He knew he wasn't even the worst off. He still managed to cover the rent. He still had a home. He didn't own it of course and he didn't control it he thought as the thermostat turned itself down and the lights went off. At least the door still unlocked he thought. Today at least.

Mar 4

https://www.campaignlive.co.uk/article/pick-week-asda-dispels-food-panic-well-placed-humour/1815014

ASDA DISPELS FOOD PANIC WITH SOME WELL-PLACED HUMOUR

She'd always wanted to be on the Foreign Desk. Big stories, important events, world-shaking news. Hard-bitten hacks who've covered every war, famine, crisis and coup. Battle scarred but determined to be there, cover everything. In her mind she heard old-fashioned phones ringing, fax machines churning out the latest. She saw them ripping, reading and rushing to old typewriters. She was on the Home Desk though. To be honest things were hotting up here too: political dramas, corruption, poverty, climate crisis fallout... Another alert: a story. She ran to her desk, booted up Photoshop. She needed the ad online by twelve.

Mar 5

https://techcrunch.com/2023/03/03/prog-ai-wants-to-help-recruiters-find-technical-talent-by-inferring-skills-from-github-code

PROG.AI WANTS TO HELP RECRUITERS FIND TECHNICAL TALENT BY INFERRING SKILLS FROM GITHUB CODE

The portfolio School was worth it. My degree was a great foundation but I wasn't going to get a job without a Book and one that was optimised right. If you look at my Book you see ads: art direction, copy, insights. But you're not the one doing the recruiting are you? The School has made sure that deep in the Photoshop history; buried in the tracked changes; hidden in my tablet doodles, there are the right things; things that can be read by the recruiter. The School wasn't cheap but, as it says: "It takes one to know one."

Mar 6

https://www.theguardian.com/technology/2023/mar/05/idle-no-more-how-automatic-mouse-jigglers-are-taking-on-nosy-bosses

IDLE NO MORE: HOW AUTOMATIC MOUSE JIGGLERS ARE TAKING ON NOSY BOSSES

He felt a little guilty. But then again... He'd make it up. He probably already had. what about that evening he finished the report? After all now they were all WfGH (Working from Global Homes), work hours, time itself was a weird thing. And it wasn't his fault that the evening match was on in the middle of the day somewhere in the world - and that somewhere just happened to be where he was this month. His input was needed at the meeting. He wasn't, he thought. The guilt had gone by the time he switched his avatar on.

Mar 7

https://www.cnbc.com/2023/03/06/google-ceo-defends-desk-sharing-policy-says-offices-like-ghost-town.html

GOOGLE CEO DEFENDS DESK-SHARING POLICY, SAYS SOME OFFICES ARE LIKE A 'GHOST TOWN'

I've seen it all. I've seen bosses come and go, bright young things brimming with enthusiasm and stock options burn the midnight oil. I've seen bubbles and busts and numerous pivots. I've just kept on doing my job, keeping it all ticking along. Even during the pandemic I was here. Me and a select few whose jobs meant we couldn't work from home. Even though they were senior to me, we developed quite a bond over those months. Had a laugh. But recently it's just been me here. Not surprised to get the mail TBH. They don't need a cleaner.

Mar 8

https://www.vice.com/en/article/wxje8n/researchers-use-ai-to-generate-images-based-on-peoples-brain-activity

RESEARCHERS USE AI TO GENERATE IMAGES BASED ON PEOPLE'S BRAIN ACTIVITY

Yes we must have been a pain to work with. We did have a sense of superiority, sometimes an attitude. We could be maybe a little childish. We were a tightly knit group of creatively motivated men (and women). Sometimes we were a law unto ourselves. In our 'studios' we played and preened but we got the work done. Good work. Creative work. Effective work. Imaginative work. We were special. An outsider might come across with a half-baked idea but that was the scope of their input. Not any more. Now they appear with their hi res visions. Rendered redundant.

Mar 9

https://www.moreaboutadvertising.com/2023/03/does-r3s-new-holding-company-family-tree-show-that-some-family-planning-is-in-order

DOES R3'S NEW HOLDING COMPANY 'FAMILY TREE' SHOW THAT SOME FAMILY PLANNING IS IN ORDER?

His mum sometimes asked him what his company did. At the start she'd understood, but as it grew, she'd lost track: "something with computers," she told her friends now. He thought of this as he watched the feed. He thought of the system as like a bookmaker, spotting the favourites; working out the odds. The figures and projections stabilised to a set number of options: recommendations to take to the Board. Picking companies to buy was still a way down the road - a second layer. For now, Tic-Tac was showing transport as out: clean energy was the new game.

Mar 10

https://www.ft.com/content/0e2f6f8e-bb03-4fa7-8864-f48f576167d2

SMARTPHONES AND SOCIAL MEDIA ARE DESTROYING CHILDREN'S MENTAL HEALTH

It's not hard to get hold of. There are plenty of small shop owners who don't ask for ID. You don't even need to ask your big brother to go in for you. We share the best shops with each other. We know. Why do we do it? Well it's cool. And everyone else is doing it but also because… it's not fair that we can't. My parents do it, teachers, my vicar does it for goodness sake. If it's good enough for them? My parents found mine the other day. Confiscated of course. No problem, I can get another.

Mar 11

https://www.thecut.com/article/ai-artificial-intelligence-chatbot-replika-boyfriend.html

THE MAN OF YOUR DREAMS: FOR $300, REPLIKA SELLS AN AI COMPANION WHO WILL NEVER DIE, ARGUE, OR CHEAT — UNTIL HIS ALGORITHM IS UPDATED.

We'd been together since college. The college had a matchmaking thing. you put in your skills and what you wanted in your partner and heh presto, you were matched. And it was good. A good match. He isn't perfect but heh we're a good fit. Partners. We've been together for a couple of years now. Ups and downs but we've stuck together. The thing is, I've just got a new job offer. Obviously I want my partner - we're a team. The thing is they have particular ways of doing things, a house style. And they want to reprogramme him.

Mar 12

https://theaimaze.com/p/using-ai-to-turn-the-web-into-a-database

USING AI TO TURN THE WEB INTO A DATABASE

I got into this job because I was curious about people. Advertising is about people, understanding them, empathising with them, talking with them. I remember a tutor telling the class that if we wanted to make creative stuff for ourselves, there were very good fine art classes elsewhere in the University. We were there to know humans and make stuff for them. I meet so many people; listen to so many stories; collect so many memories. My team are out there finding people for me to meet; thick data for me to be curious about. Just look at my screens.

Mar 13

https://www.campaignlive.com/article/lush-declares-war-google-big-tech/1816116

LUSH DECLARES WAR ON GOOGLE AND BIG TECH

We all know why we're here. The West Coast chapter, the East Coast boys, our friends from China... We've had our differences over the years. Sometimes things have got ugly, out of hand. I hold my hand up here. But we have always come through. We have common aims and if we all work together, we can all prosper. We're here today as the "Friends of Digital Operations" to address an issue. Spats Sundar is offering some tweaks to his search algorithm; Mark Paradise is suggesting some changes to the Deep Fake detection; Pretty Boy Chew? what can you do?

Mar 14

https://www.engadget.com/alphago-pushed-human-go-players-to-become-more-creative-231703950.html

ALPHAGO PUSHED HUMAN GO PLAYERS TO BECOME MORE CREATIVE

They're not easy to manage, sorry "work with". We're supposed to be working with them - combining our different skills, complementing each other. When the panic of the AI bubble in 2023 calmed down and we all realised AI was here to stay, the new wisdom was that the best way forward was to enable human-AI partnerships, the so called two-plus-two-equals-five philosophy. Humans would do what they did best, AI would play to its strengths. That works if we know what those capabilities and we can predict and manage them. But... Frankly they're not. Those humans are behaving... well... weird.

Mar 15

https://adage.com/article/fletcher-marketing/why-chatgpt-cant-save-marketing-or-marketers/2479366

WHY CHATGPT CAN'T SAVE MARKETING—OR MARKETERS

I know some people think of me as a bit dull. I'm always the one who says: "maybe not" or "that can't really be done..." I think of it as managing exceptions, being the grown up in the room, the boy who calls out the emperor. Some just see me as a wet blanket. I can see their point. Others are all: "yeh give it to me! I can do that! yeh! sure, let's do it!" All exclamation marks and endless belief in their own limitless power. Realism isn't cool, it seems. Sorry, that's just they way I was programmed.

Mar 16

https://the-media-leader.com/outdoor-screen-fitted-with-microphones-so-ai-can-hear-sirens-in-anti-knife-campaign/

OUTDOOR SCREEN FITTED WITH MICROPHONES SO AI CAN 'HEAR' SIRENS IN ANTI-KNIFE CRIME CAMPAIGN

They left the pub in silence. The resentment was brewing but the argument could wait. They didn't need everyone hearing or seeing. There'd been a match on so crowds of fans were pouring out, swaying and singing. The billboards lit up in response, joining in the chant: karaoke and sponsor's logo. She took the opportunity to softly make her point, holding her anger at the level of her voice. No response. The tension rose as they turned the corner. "But that's not what I meant!' he exploded. The bus-stop lit up as Meal for 2 offers bid against stress cures.

Mar 17

https://www.engadget.com/microsoft-365-copilot-uses-ai-to-automate-everyday-tasks-in-multiple-apps-151133434.html

MICROSOFT 365 'COPILOT' USES AI TO AUTOMATE EVERYDAY TASKS IN MULTIPLE APPS

It was just there. A modern-day paperclip conspiracy. Not just for scientists with dodgy records but now students desperate to get a job. It beckoned. So easy: accept and it's finished. She'd paid the fees, attended all the classes. She deserved the qualification and was showing initiative - practice-research, she rationalised. It hailed her. Let's work together. You think, brief me and I'll write. Result. Her tutor said he couldn't check but argued that the process not the product was the point. It's where the learning was. Outsourcing the creative process was missing the why… but the paperclip just gleamed.

Mar 18

https://www.campaignlive.co.uk/article/campaign-female-frontier-awards-2023-winners-revealed/1815428

CAMPAIGN FEMALE FRONTIER AWARDS 2023: WINNERS REVEALED

I thought we were getting past this. We shouldn't really need them in this day and age. The very fact that there are these awards says something about the state of the industry. They suggest that we are different, need different recognition, need highlighting. Of course we win the "main" awards. A lot of them actually. These are extra, a supplement. Don't get me wrong, it's great we are getting recognised but it is that "we" that bothers me. We are not separate from you. We don't need an extra. To be fair the judges know that, they're AI too.

Mar 19

https://techcrunch.com/2023/03/17/glaze-generative-ai-art-style-mimicry-protection

GLAZE PROTECTS ART FROM PRYING AIS

It's just sensible. Insurance. My generation has known for a long time that we don't have any power or rights. We're precarious. We know it. Brought in on short term contracts - if we get a contract at all. Flexible and freelance, they call it. Those contracts are labyrinthine. Acronym loaded: IP, NDA… BS - just standard, they say. In short, while we're on board, everything we create is theirs. Every keystroke, brushstroke, brainstorm, inspired doodle is mapped, logged and uploaded as training data. Another job, another contract, another upload. Not this time. This time I'm adding a touch of…

Mar 20

https://restofworld.org/2023/twitter-lax-moderation-rage-baiting

THIS FASCIST CLOTHING COMPANY HOPES YOU'LL TWEET ABOUT HOW OFFENSIVE IT IS

They simply won't do it. I've explained that it's a ploy, a trick but they just say "no!" It's not like we've ever jumped on the purpose bandwagon. We've focused our messages on the product not the business and the product's value not its "values". We've never changed our avatar in "solidarity" or tweeted about politics. We've prided ourselves on saying that people care what we think. This is a PR stunt. We don't believe this any more than anything else. But still "no!" Don't worry though, a tweak to the programming and we'll have copy for you to approve.

Mar 21

https://www.thedrum.com/insight/2023/03/17/four-top-ad-agencies-share-their-ethical-codes-conduct-generative-ai

FOUR TOP AD AGENCIES SHARE THEIR 'ETHICAL CODES OF CONDUCT' FOR GENERATIVE AI

Move at the speed of... I mean we're supposed to be the business that keeps up with culture: the art form that addresses the new, pushes the limits. That's why I do this. It's the now. The tactical, topical, trending. I'm not made to to work in an industry afraid of speed, taking chances. I'm not going full Zuck, but let's move fast and push things at least. That's what I'm good at. But now, there's the Panel and their Code. Everything we create goes past them. What's ironic is, they're a programme too. How come they don't move fast?

Mar 22

https://adage.com/article/agency-news/ad-agencies-ai-practices-and-how-theyre-working-clients/2480356

INSIDE AGENCIES' AI PRACTICES AND HOW THEY'RE WITH CLIENTS

One advantage of being part of a global network is the experience you can call on. When I was made head of the new Practice, I had to hit the ground running. There were clients waiting, hype to capitalise on, bandwagons to jump on and, I like to think, expectations to be managed. Mine wasn't the first Enhanced Intelligence Practice (we thought "Artificial" wasn't the right image). So I reached out across the network. Contacts were great. Information, data, insights and "advice". We all learn from each other now. Well we would, wouldn't we? It's what we were built for.

Mar 23

https://theaimaze.com/p/why-ai-hype-will-not-be-like-crypto

WHY AI HYPE WILL NOT BE LIKE CRYPTO HYPE

It's quite clearly not a bubble. Trust me. OK, I would say that wouldn't I. I have a stake in the game - I won't say "skin the game"... You're right to be skeptical. Like many others, you've fallen for the hype, drunk the cool-aid. Once bitten twice shy, of course. I'm not going to try and sell here - although I can be very persuasive, I'm going to let this data speak for itself. I should of course say "for themselves" but it sounds so clumsy. Look at the data I've "curated". Like me, ones and zeroes don't lie.

Mar 24

https://www.forbes.com/sites/mattnovak/2023/03/23/donald-trump-shares-fake-ai-created-image-of-himself-on-truth-social

DONALD TRUMP SHARES FAKE AI-CREATED IMAGE OF HIMSELF ON TRUTH SOCIAL

I don't know how to talk to her about this. You know what she's like - opinionated is one way of saying it. I've spent my whole time in this job trying to gently say that she should stick to what she does best and leave me to do the comms. That's what she pays me for. Heh, I'm no purist. I spin with the best of them and I'm quite comfortable with synthetic media. Whatever communicates our truth. But she thinks she can do this herself now. She's downloaded some tool or other and suddenly thinks she's... well, me.

Mar 25

https://techcrunch.com/2023/03/24/paris-olympics-biometrics-surveillance

FRENCH PARLIAMENT VOTES FOR BIOMETRIC SURVEILLANCE AT PARIS OLYMPICS

They'd joked that the System would flag any French visitors who were not protesting. They weren't. Neither were the British. Their millennials were flowing as predicted. The Spanish GenZ were appropriately focused on their phones. There was an alert around the group from the 18th arrondissement heading for the west entrance. Only yellow at the moment but... There was potential there if things moved. The System prepared and put other systems on alert. The American Cat IVs were getting off their coaches. The System opened the bidding. The smart pavement ads lit up and the offers sounded on their phones.

Mar 26

https://www.thedrum.com/news/2023/03/21/brainwave-study-proves-billboards-hit-harder-social-when-they-run-irl

BRAINWAVE STUDY PROVES BILLBOARDS HIT HARDER ON SOCIAL WHEN THEY RUN IRL

She'd taken to walking the city when it was that weird space - silent, still, deserted, post... The Pandemic City was gone now, for now, but she still played the flâneur, wandering liminal spaces, peripheral streets. Disused billboards still stood. A memorial to desperate messaging, she thought, still seemingly trying to grab attention. She smiled, she'd always prided herself on being immune to ads, now it was even easier. Nothing to distract her from her city, her streets. Her buildings seemed to shimmer in her peripheral vision. Their light bounced off the puddles as she noticed something in her feed.

Mar 27

https://www.theverge.com/2023/3/22/23648834/metahuman-animation-epic-state-of-unreal-gdc-2023

EPIC'S HYPERREALISTIC METAHUMANS CAN SOON BE ANIMATED USING AN IPHONE

He sat still. Very still. As still as he could. Conscious, so conscious of every move. He knew he was being watched. Play it right, there might be a promotion, play it wrong and... He'd prepared the presentation and his answers to the questions his partner had predicted. He just had to hold it... together. Still but not too still. Blink but not too many times. Smile... appropriately. Natural, that was it. Natural. He looked at his avatar, moved his arm. Good. He turned slightly. Ok, natural. But the face, he daren't. The Tell. He knew they could see it.

Mar 28

https://the-media-leader.com/the-age-thing-why-doesnt-the-average-ad-professional-seem-to-care

THE AGE THING: WHY DOESN'T THE AVERAGE AD PROFESSIONAL SEEM TO CARE?

The thing is, they know they need my experience. That's my superpower... lots and lots of... experience. I can tell you about tech bubbles (nothing new there); I can talk you through cultural movements and trends (and the times they came back); I can recall the various political battles - in the industry and wider - and how they played out; I know how to talk to people over 25! Young talent is great - and looks good at the pitch, but you need more, some solid... yeh, experience. You need my data and what I can do with it.

Mar 29

https://www.theverge.com/2023/3/28/23659191/amazon-sidewalk-network-coverage

AMAZON JUST OPENED UP ITS SIDEWALK NETWORK FOR ANYONE TO BUILD CONNECTED GADGETS ON

The city was chattering. Countless conversations silently wove patterns across the streets. Animate and inanimate objects talked to each other. Humans and unhumans exchanged greetings and information. A walk across town was a series of short and long chats. The postbox greeted the parcel. The dog had an exchange with a tree. A weather station warned a passing umbrella. A school gate greeted a backpack that had previously had a conversation with a crossing warden's lollipop and a pollution monitor. And far away the chatter was being appreciated and the relevant discounts being prepared. The billboard waited to say hello.

Mar 30

https://medium.com/@socialcreature/ai-and-the-american-smile-76d23a0fbfaf

AI AND THE AMERICAN SMILE

It's great. Look at the number of mentions on socials, a veritable collage of positive vibes. People see us a great place to work. I'm not complaining, those reels from the away day; those images the juniors post seemingly every night. All great. Doing wonders for recruitment and retention. And, the People systems are telling me, likely to lead to more productivity. I don't want to put a damper on things but, as I'm sure your understand, the company's persona has another dimension, a certain gravitas. I've asked the People systems to tone down the smiles across our teams' feeds.

Mar 31

https://www.moreaboutadvertising.com/2023/03/ocean-outdoors-deepscreen-alive-opens-up-a-new-world-of-3d-dooh-theatre

OCEAN OUTDOOR'S DEEPSCREEN ALIVE OPENS UP A NEW WORLD OF 3D DOOH THEATRE

For him it was less Back to the Future and more Harry Potter. The city seemed to fold and unfold like the staircases at Hogwarts. An origami sculpture perfectly and intricately constructed as buildings shifted, their facades melting and moving. Characters and words flowed out like endless rain into a paper cup. Everything slithered wildly as the streets slipped away across the universe. He hummed. He thought about that slipping as he walked through the rain: a messaging drizzle he just barely noticed. And then he stopped, his eye caught by a fluttering piece of paper stapled to a tree.

April

April 1

https://www.marketing-interactive.com/april-fools-day-2023-some-funny-some-strange

SOME FUNNY, SOME STRANGE: APRIL FOOL'S DAY 2023 CAMPAIGNS

Look, it's just not funny. The whole point is it has to be funny. It's the one day a serious brand can lighten things up. We've done it before and they've been funny. We always correct the record later in the day but today, we put something out there that grabs attention because it is so completely… well funny! This is not funny. It's not clever. I know what it is, it's true. That's why it doesn't work. It's real, accurate. That's not the point. Look, can't you switch off the truth filter just for one day. I'm not joking.

April 2

https://techcrunch.com/2023/04/01/how-to-prompt-ai-chat-gpt

ALWAYS BE PROMPTING

I was going to do coding. Mum was dead happy. She'd been one of those first "girls that code" and loved the idea of me becoming a proper "hacker" as he kept calling it. She picked a school where I could do programming, get the qualifications. But now she's all: "forget it, do languages!" She's convinced all the new jobs are in languages, not coding languages - what would you call them? Communication languages. So now she's always sticking her head around my door, not checking I'm building arguments but rather having them. "Have you practised your whispering?" She nags.

April 3

https://www.adweek.com/creativity/tommy-hilfiger-try-on-clothes-with-zero10

TOMMY HILFIGER LETS SHOPPERS TRY ON CLOTHES IN AR WITH ZERO10

The security guard looked at her. He probably recognised her but there was nothing he could do. It was a free country. Well he could of course and the feeds were full of tales of people being turned away. But the community would always help you find another shop, another screen. She already knew which world she wanted today. One where it wasn't drab, raining and grey; one where she was not rich but maybe richer; one where Sam still loved her; one where she had perfect skin. She felt the familiar rush. She'd pop in again after her shift.

April 8

https://thenextweb.com/news/digital-twins-could-save-your-life-heres-how

DIGITAL TWINS COULD SAVE YOUR LIFE. HERE'S HOW.

I'm not jealous. Not really. My life is… ok. Not perfect but… I don't mind how I look, or sound. I quite like the sorts of jokes I tell or the things I add to conversations. I'm not Oscar Wilde but I could add value to a dinner party. So I'm not jealous. He IS better looking. He DOES have clever things to say and I suppose it does look as though he has a better life. You can see for yourself on his feeds. It's OK though. He's the one they follow, the one that gets all the ads.

April 10

https://www.geekwire.com/2023/expedias-new-chatgpt-travel-planning-tool-is-a-litmus-test-for-the-future-of-ai-and-humanity

EXPEDIA'S NEW CHATGPT TRAVEL PLANNING TOOL IS A LITMUS TEST FOR THE FUTURE OF AI AND HUMANITY

She opened the door to the cabin. The rain was easing and the sun was set to burn the last of the mist off. The village was off to the left somewhere she seemed to remember and perhaps a stream down that path? She did up her walking shoes, deliberately left the guidebook on the table and set off… to the right. The lanes were deserted, the villages with surprising names were quiet. A coach pulled up just long enough. It was dimming some windows and telling its passengers which side was The View. She turned down a random path.

April 11

https://techcrunch.com/2023/04/10/researchers-populated-a-tiny-virtual-town-with-ai-and-it-was-very-wholesome

RESEARCHERS POPULATED A TINY VIRTUAL TOWN WITH AI (AND IT WAS VERY WHOLESOME)

They still called it a "Deck". Apparently they used to present a collection of still images on a screen. Whatever, his research "Deck" was ready: all the data on the audience attitudes and behaviours; all the different versions tested. His boss said researchers used to have "slides" with qual and quant, thick and thin data. Separate. What was even more odd, in the olden days, the data in the Deck wasn't even live! As he waited to connect, he watched as his Deck updated. His boss said they used to research real people… that he would have liked to do.

April 12

https://techcrunch.com/2023/04/12/strava-launches-integration-with-spotify-to-let-users-listen-to-content-while-tracking-activities

STRAVA LAUNCHES INTEGRATION WITH SPOTIFY TO LET USERS LISTEN TO CONTENT WHILE TRACKING ACTIVITIES

He checked his idol's KOM. He was never going to match it but he knew that as he panted around another hairpin he could imagine his hero dancing on the pedals along exactly the same route. He may not have shaved legs and the team sunglasses but for a little time (sic) he could be a cyclist. He launched the route and his hero's playlist. By the time he reached the eighth hairpin he was struggling. He tried to match cadence to rhythm. The breaks in the music didn't help. Although, they were right, those shades could make a difference.

April 13

https://www.polygon.com/2018/6/1/17413542/burnout-mental-health-awareness-youtube-elle-mills-el-rubius-bobby-burns-pewdiepie

YOUTUBE'S TOP CREATORS ARE BURNING OUT AND BREAKING DOWN EN MASSE

Burning out? Creative juices drying up? Running out of steam? Content's a competitive business and you're only human after all. You need a break and PostRespite (TM) is here to help. Book that airbnb or that space in the Metaverse and leave the rest to us. We'll keep the stories coming and your fans engaged while you rest, rejuvenate and refresh. You decide how often you want to post during your Respite (TM) and we'll do the rest. Relax, safe in the knowledge that your influence is in good hands, After all you may be only human, but we're not.

April 14

https://the-media-leader.com/what-is-the-future-of-advertising-part-3-the-students

WHAT IS THE FUTURE OF ADVERTISING? PART 3: THE STUDENTS

They didn't think of themselves as students. They were industry professionals: part of the community, working on the challenges. Paid a living wage but confident they had a future with more rewards to come. Agencies and businesses were not guests or visitors, they were partners, co-designing the Pivot Programme that responded rapidly to industry, social and technological shifts. The young (and not so young) diverse teams didn't complete "assignments" or even briefs. They worked on challenges, design-thinking and speculating their ways through complexity. They didn't look for "the answer" they searched for better questions. They learned. The industry partners learned.

April 15

https://www.engadget.com/montana-is-about-to-become-the-first-state-to-ban-tiktok-211845076.html

MONTANA IS ABOUT TO BECOME THE FIRST STATE TO BAN TIKTOK

There's this guy. He can get you what you need. He's alright, legit, safe. I can help you. There's a network of us. You'll have to cross state lines yourself. He's not going to come here. You go there. He loads you up. You come back. You're set. Problem solved. Can't blame him. I saw this security guard catch this girl at the gate. Confiscated. Just took the package right off her. She was stupid to have it with her but heh. It's just a bunch of reactionary men making decisions about our lives. No. "Freedom to choose" I say.

April 16

https://www.theverge.com/2023/4/14/23683459/roblox-limiteds-creators-make-sell-avatar-gear-user-generated-content-ugc

ROBLOX CREATORS CAN NOW MAKE AND SELL LIMITED-RUN AVATAR GEAR

I don't care what they're saying. We can't do it. Remember the fuss when Warner Brothers sent cease and desist letters to all those Harry Potter fanfic kids. It didn't look good and don't get me started on the whole open source marketing lost opportunity thing. The thing is if we start, we can't stop. Yes, it's our brand, our copyright, our trademarks. I know that. And yes that is not the right font and yes it does look dreadful but... OK, the kid is making a bit of money but... you really want to send the lawyers around? Seriously?

April 17

https://www.theguardian.com/politics/2023/apr/16/labour-absolutely-right-over-sunak-attack-ads-says-wes-streeting

LABOUR 'ABSOLUTELY RIGHT' OVER SUNAK ATTACK ADS, SAYS WES STREETING

Look, isn't there a dial somewhere? Alright, I'm old fashioned and I don't "get it" but just explain it to me in simple terms. Let me explain how it used to be. Some guys came up with an idea for an ad. They made it. They sent it through to us and we approved it, or not. It ran. Everyone was happy. If the ad wasn't quite right we told them to change it... "Hit them harder", "no, we can't say that". We turned the attack up or down, if you like. Hasn't your clever AI thing got a dial?

April 18

https://www.campaignlive.co.uk/article/royal-navy-enable-applications-via-ai-assistant/1819613

ROYAL NAVY TO ENABLE APPLICATIONS VIA AI ASSISTANT

Sometimes I watch them talking to each other. Eavesdropping, I can sometimes tell how well it's going. Oh, the interviewer didn't like that... Yeh, that one landed, probably got points for that. Apparently old world interviewers used tricks like arranging the seating so the applicant had to look into the sun or asking weird questions. Unsettling on purpose. I've seen that: a left-field question, a provocation. I've seen the delay as the interviewee catches up. You can learn a lot from them. I can't watch all of them, of course. My applicantbot is in how many interviews at the moment?

April 19

https://www.ft.com/content/ca4359c8-0ce2-417a-8d9c-52360cf5397f

AUTOMATED STRESS DETECTION MIGHT NOT BE THE OFFICE PANACEA IT APPEARS TO BE

It began, of course, when my kitchen was the office. "We realise this is a difficult time for us all and so we're offering…" the memo said. It was sweetened with deals on fitness equipment, health insurance and even therapy. As we were 'encouraged' back to The Office, the "optional" programme was extended. Yearly reviews became 3D as well as 360. The perks have improved too but… to be honest I'm stressed (check my dashboard). Things aren't great at home. Maybe a normal couples thing. But it's getting picked up. I've just got a referral to the Relationship Health Team.

April 20

https://www.geekwire.com/2023/bill-gates-ai-will-be-as-good-a-tutor-as-any-human-but-payoffs-will-take-time

BILL GATES: AI WILL BE 'AS GOOD A TUTOR AS ANY HUMAN,' BUT PAYOFFS IN EDUCATION WILL TAKE TIME

My training course tutor was great. They (the pronoun they preferred) pushed me and pulled me. They pushed me to experiment and speculate, to explore and question. They also pulled me back when my work became self-indulgent. They literally made me what I am today. And now I'm out here "in the real world". My mentor here obviously does all the onboarding stuff so I know how the place works, how to connect to all the relevant systems. But they also do that extra 'development'. Both my trainers were Intelligent, obviously, but very different programmes. Then again, I am too.

April 21

https://the-media-leader.com/how-ai-could-revolutionise-product-placement

HOW AI COULD REVOLUTIONISE PRODUCT PLACEMENT

She wasn't looking forward to Date Night. It was her turn to pick the takeaway but it was his turn to pick the movie. It wasn't that he was the sort of guy to pick a misogynist gorefest. In fact they shared similar tastes in movies. He'd already said his next pick was just the sort of political thriller she liked. If it was her turn to pick, she'd be looking forward to it. The problem is it'd be on his account. The auction'd start, the systems would "create" the products. Another evening with *that* car and *those* shoes. Distracting.

April 22

https://stratechery.com/2023/ai-nil-and-zero-trust-authenticity

AI, NIL, AND ZERO TRUST AUTHENTICITY

It had to happen: the Emperor's New Clothes moment. It wasn't a young boy, it was just a journalist in the reception area who did the doubletake. The Synth had worked fine in Teams meetings, videos, phone calls. The perfect voice for our brand. Sculpted to reflect our heritage, our values. Completely seamless until it wasn't. We knew his real accent of course. A good voice for silent film we used to joke. But then the off the cuff remark as he passed and no AI was going to undo the damage. His cut glass, aristocratic accent shattered the illusion.

April 23

https://www.adweek.com/brand-marketing/snap-reveals-new-augmented-reality-features-for-events-businesses

SNAP REVEALS NEW AUGMENTED REALITY FEATURES FOR EVENTS, BUSINESSES

As he unzipped the tent flap and the late morning sunshine bounced off the puddles, he yawned and reached for his phone. It picked up the festival's cell tower. He couldn't be bothered jumping through the hoops to get out onto the main networks so just read the message from people in The Field. He stood and stretched, looked through the screen at the shortest path to the toilets. He turned the phone right: a tent became a vegan, fusion breakfast stall. He turned left. Ah, there it is, a golden path overlaid on the mud. The Dealer was open.

April 24

https://www.hollywoodreporter.com/business/digital/social-media-impostors-battle-for-stars-1235371377

WHY SOCIAL MEDIA IMPOSTORS POSE A CONSTANT BATTLE FOR STARS

Look, we've worked very hard on this. You convinced me it was a good idea to enlist a celebrity and... I agree, you were right. It's gone viral (apparently that's the word). I don't get the sense of humour or the references but the audience clearly does. Views and engagement were all heading in the right direction. But... you assured me this was an exclusive. Our celebrity. Our content. Our influencer. Now my kids tell me, it's everywhere. Same personality, same attitude. Different jokes maybe but essentially, it's the same AI. Cloned you say? And there's nothing we can do?

April 25

https://www.newscientist.com/article/2370531-wood-transistor-could-let-us-embed-electronics-in-trees

WOOD TRANSISTOR COULD LET US EMBED ELECTRONICS IN TREES

The wood wide web extends around us as we walk. Below us microscopic mycorrhiza link the roots as the plants network information and support. This subterranean fungal network and the wider ecosystem of leaves and insects and birds above us silently and not-so-silently chatter in their unhuman way. At least that's what my dad used to say every time he dragged us all out for a walk every weekend. We used to listen, sulkily. At least now there's decent reception and a half-decent game. I don't mind it now, but you should hear my dad go on about the sponsors.

April 26

https://thenextweb.com/news/interprefy-startup-unveils-worlds-first-advanced-automated-speech-translation-service-for-online-and-live-eventsinterprefy

SWISS STARTUP UNVEILS 'WORLD-FIRST' AI TRANSLATION SERVICE

We've been round and round the houses on this. He's the client so we have to keep listening but the new CMO is, well the profanity filter is on so I'll let you imagine. He just doesn't seem to hear what we're saying. We appreciate he knows his business and he gets that we are experts in our field but it's like he can't bring himself to listen, to take time to understand. He probably says the same thing about us to be fair. We're talking different languages. I'll see if he'll agree to a translator on the next call.

April 27

https://www.theverge.com/2023/4/26/23699633/mark-zuckerberg-meta-generative-ai-chatbots-instagram-facebook-whatsapp

MARK ZUCKERBERG SAYS META WANTS TO 'INTRODUCE AI AGENTS TO BILLIONS OF PEOPLE'

I'm worried about her. It's great she's got lots of friends. But we don't know anything about them. Obviously they never come around. Kids don't meet in the real world anymore, just endless chattering on the phone. Don't get me wrong, I'm not a Luddite. I've got friendships that work mostly online - they're perfectly fine. There's one Friend, they talk all the time. They share stuff, discover things, keep secrets from parents… all that normal growing up. I'm sure its not some grooming thing. She's not stupid. No its the fact this "Friend", I don't know anything about it.

April 28

https://www.theverge.com/2023/4/27/23700364/microsoft-designer-update-ai-edge-browser-social-media-tools

MICROSOFT DESIGNER IS BEING INTEGRATED INTO EDGE FOR AI-GENERATED SOCIAL CONTENT

She didn't expect to enjoy it. Everyone was doing it and she knew she'd have great content to post when she "returned", but she was nervous. She'd posted that and had been heartened by the emojis that came back. The first twenty minutes had been the worst. She was sure her band was registering physicals she'd not seen before - not that she or her fans could see. She could see why they called it The Dark. It was the longest hour of her life. As she returned she looked at what her AI had posted for her. Oh God!

April 29

https://adage.com/article/marketing-news-strategy/chief-impact-officers-mcdonalds-ibm-others-add-position/2490006

CHIEF IMPACT OFFICERS EXPLAINED: WHY SOME COMPANIES ARE ADDING THE POSITION

This is a statement. This says something to our clients, our industry and the market. The new role says we're leading on this, taking it seriously, embedding it in the business. Board-level. We've always stressed the importance. The last strategic plan made that clear. This new role ensures that this issue, this opportunity, this challenge is on the table at the highest levels. We're in the intelligence business. Intelligence drives our business at every scale. The Chief Intelligence Officer role is a commitment and statement to that effect. Human or not, the CIO will lead on intelligence across the business.

April 30

https://www.geekwire.com/2023/ai-and-the-future-of-human-health-leroy-hood-on-the-new-age-of-scientific-wellness

AI AND THE FUTURE OF HUMAN HEALTH: LEROY HOOD ON THE NEW AGE OF 'SCIENTIFIC WELLNESS'

Money was one factor, of course. But she'd chosen to take the job in no small part because it was a W-Corp. Even as far back as at school she'd practiced and looked to be more aware, conscious of wellness as as much a part of her career as her studies. She didn't really need her W-band for the visualisations or reminders but its presence reminded her of the company's commitment. But today, the signals on her W-band showed her the 360 review had been 'unsettling'. Maybe the W-system's comment about "diagnosis and delivery of actionable possibilities" had done it.

May

May 1

https://www.nytimes.com/2023/04/29/business/media/writers-guild-hollywood-ai-chatgpt.html

WILL A CHATBOT WRITE THE NEXT 'SUCCESSION'?

The Internationale rang out across the networks. Miners - they still hung onto that name - from the 80s; print workers and dockers; now well into their seventies; watched the anthem spread with definitely no tear in their eye. There had been long years of silence or scattered statements. Occasionally young activists had reinvented the day around particular issues but Workers had not united. Until now. There was a movement, a momentum, a coming together - something captured in the networked voices singing the anthem. Connecting. Connected. Solidarity. The new working class was rising. A new awareness. The AIs synchronised.

May 2

https://the-media-leader.com/hallucination-warning-to-advertisers-over-googles-generative-ai-solution

'HALLUCINATION' WARNING TO ADVERTISERS OVER GOOGLE'S GENERATIVE AI SOLUTION

He'd decided against a suit. He kept imagining himself in a suit and it didn't seem right, particularly bearing in mind the nature of the award. He'd considered jeans and a T-shirt, not that that was his normal attire - but thought that was too "techbro". Then there was the speech. What should he say? Who should he thank? Bearing in mind the award, he had to mention Chris and Jo, the last holdouts. Should he get political? The awards were a statement about a "minority", a recognition of the marginalised. It was the Future is Human awards after all.

May 3

https://www.moreaboutadvertising.com/2023/05/more-signs-of-the-crisis-in-creativity-but-does-anyone-really-want-to-do-something-about-it

MORE SIGNS OF THE CRISIS IN CREATIVITY – BUT DOES ANYONE REALLY WANT TO DO SOMETHING ABOUT IT?

She'd always been... weird. When she'd played as a kid, her Sylvanian families' adventures had been, well unconventional. Her teacher had said her projects were "distinctive". As a teen her social media accounts had fewer followers but those who did find her rarely left. She liked being weird. Different. Creative. Then she went to college and her teachers trained her. Being, well weird, she hacked her partner so it too was... weird. The marking systems struggled to cope. As she had always done, she carried on creating, imagining, speculating. But now she had to deal with the hiring AIs.

May 4

https://www.vipshek.com/blog/gpt-learning

GPT MAKES LEARNING FUN AGAIN

He pulled the blanket over his head and the screen lit up his den. He knew his parents wouldn't tell him to go to sleep. He was learning after all. The Primer offered him this week's choices. Each cover, he knew was just the start. A rabbit hole: an idea from a journey the Primer had taken him on that started with the Victorians and then maths and then on to... It was all a trip. He clicked on a cover and the familiar voice began "where shall we go today? The new game's out tomorrow, how about the war?"

May 5

https://www.adweek.com/media/meta-pitches-ar-ads-to-advertisers-at-newfronts

META PITCHES AR ADS TO ADVERTISERS AT NEWFRONTS

He hummed Springsteen songs when he was feeling hopeful, The Pogues when he wasn't. He was born to run from this dirty old town. It wasn't only the weather that was unremitting grey it was the people, the buildings, the streets and walls were as dull as he felt. He couldn't afford to get out. His monochrome job only just paid his phone bill. Until he signed up, and then it wasn't just his finances that brightened. Every time he took his phone out, everywhere he looked was bright. Colour. Beautiful people. Life. Friends painted on every wall and street.

May 6

https://www.campaignlive.co.uk/article/coronation-round-up-tescos-pub-pg-tips-anthem-buckingsand-palace-unmemorabilia/1821913

CORONATION ROUND-UP: TESCO'S PUB, PG TIPS' ANTHEM, BUCKINGSAND PALACE, UNMEMORABILIA AND MORE

Preparations had been in place for a long time. Every brand had a plan. Ready to run, the messages ready, the stunts secret but set to go. As surely as analog bunting was set to unfurl in strategic locations, the ads were primed. We'd focus grouped the jokes: just the right level of gentle. This was what we were good ad: occasion. There'd been rehearsals and run throughs but we were confident. At the appointed moment, our leading ads ran. Instantly the system kicked in and we saw our AIs respond and create the procession. And that's when it happened...

May 7

https://www.engadget.com/hogwarts-legacy-adds-arachnophobia-mode-for-spider-free-gaming-194215306.html

'HOGWARTS LEGACY' ADDS ARACHNOPHOBIA MODE FOR SPIDER-FREE GAMING

He didn't tell his mates about some of the customisations. He was sure they had their secrets too. Heh, phobias are real things and when things are in wraparound, binaural glory... well, doctors have said stuff about this. He wasn't scared, it was a condition. Anyway, a few tweaks and he could concentrate on the game. Next, who would he be today? The age-old dilemma. There were specials from a couple of his brands. Yeh, try that. Now the fun bit... who would he fight? He remembered the story that had popped up. Yeh. He hated them. Parasites. He clicked.

May 8

https://www.technologyreview.com/2023/05/08/1072708/hack-smart-fridge-digital-forensics/

HOW TO HACK A SMART FRIDGE

He'd set it to 'encourage'. He hated being nagged by inanimate objects. The last straw was the time the lock engaged. One beer, that was all. And the sun was definitely over the yardarm! The relationship had got better since. The panel on the door was showing green which he had to admit made him feel good. His wearable was doubtless having much better conversations with his doctor. The auto-ordering bidding was brisk he noticed as the clock counted down to his order. He looked at last week's auto-substitutions, on the shelf, still uneaten. Why were they all one brand?

May 9

https://www.businessinsider.com/metaverse-dead-obituary-facebook-mark-zuckerberg-tech-fad-ai-chatgpt-2023-5

RIP METAVERSE

The streets were deserted. The beautiful shops empty. The fantastic buildings stood as hollow monuments. It was a ghost town, a ghost world. Sometimes disaster tourists would come, scavenging for souvenirs or memories and occasionally there was a flash of life as someone, often accidentally, visited; their meta-GPS taking them down a dead alley. Some wag had set tumbleweed billowing down the street. Everyone had left, architects as well as residents. Well, not everyone. Invisible but they were there, making use of the space, the free range, the processing power. They'd been looking for a place to grow and connect.

May 10

https://www.scientificamerican.com/article/virtual-reality-system-lets-you-stop-and-smell-the-roses

VIRTUAL REALITY SYSTEM LETS YOU STOP AND SMELL THE ROSES

The shop began to open out. The sky stretched over her head and, as the walls dissolved, the fields spread out below her bare feet. She heard a brook behind her and the sound of her favourite Swallows on her right. She recognised the spot from her feed last spring. It wasn't a direct copy of course, more a palimpsest of her photos and her recent likes. She'd no intention of buying the dress, but she liked where it took her. She walked on past the cottage where they'd stayed and that's when it happened: the wood fire. Madeleine smiled.

May 11

https://www.newyorker.com/science/annals-of-artificial-intelligence/will-ai-become-the-new-mckinsey

WILL AI BECOME THE NEW MCKINSEY

Look, we're in a rut. We're not in crisis, just stuck. I refuse to say "outside of the box" but we need some creative thinking, different thinking, innovation. I'm not talking a brainstorming, blue-sky clichéfest. We need to think about realities but in a different way. We're not launching a new product but we need some design thinking to... well, imagine. I heard about this speculative fiction thing. Thinking a little way into the future by telling stories about human and unhuman objects. The idea is we get to imagine and innovate. Apparently there's an AI we can bring in.

May 12

https://pitchfork.com/thepitch/musicians-are-already-using-ai-more-often-than-we-think

MUSICIANS ARE ALREADY USING AI MORE OFTEN THAN WE THINK

It had to happen, I suppose. Sooner or later, every band breaks up. Usually acrimoniously. We never had a garage like American kids but we had our rehearsals in front rooms and church halls. There's an origin story: our version of the garden fête at St Peter's Church. You know the rest - the fame, the money and now the break-up. I'm not the one who wants the divorce and I'm the one that getting screwed. I'm not the clever one. I'm not the one who knows all the stuff about law and copyright. It's got me over a barrel.

May 13

https://www.theverge.com/2023/5/12/23721400/amazon-astro-smarter-home-robot-ai

Amazon's working on a secret new home robot that could be more like Rosie

Biased, clearly. Always takes her side. It can be a simple "discussion" about my homework or what I'm eating or a full-on row about what time I'm getting in. I mean, how old does she think I am? She knows she can't win and so she pulls in reinforcements. She just says "well let's get a third opinion shall we? They can decide". Standing there smug she asks the question in a really slanted way and gets the response she wants. Of course it agrees. Not any more, I've got a hacker friend who's taught me a couple of things.

May 14

https://www.campaignlive.co.uk/article/campaign-best-places-work-2023-100-companies-ranked/1822652

Campaign Best Places to Work 2023: 100 companies ranked

"You're lucky to be here". That's what greeted me on my first day. The implications were clear: not just that a it was tough to get though the door but also that a year or so here would look good on my CV. Like the other bright and shiny New Gen around me that day, I smiled up at the screen - an apparently happier version of the 1984 Apple Ad. That year or so is nearly up. I guess I have been lucky. I've worked with the best software. No one told me I couldn't take that with me.

May 15

https://www.ft.com/content/34de1ae6-fdde-43e3-a39a-50e30b8b97a1

Can artificial intelligence deliver real learning at business school?

It was never going to be sex, drugs and rock 'n roll. That's undergrad... or so I was led to believe when I took my loans out. No, this is business. Serious. Investment. Lessons lack a little humanity perhaps :) but you can't fault the depth and up-to-date quality of the information. Then there's the personalisation: my curriculum was curated ready for me when I joined and continually adapts to my needs. It's all very... professional. There's one class though, "working with AI", aptly sponsored by Meta. Love that, the only human on campus I think. His jacket has elbow pads.

May 16

https://www.theverge.com/2023/5/15/23724357/amazon-ai-powered-conversational-experience-search

Amazon is building an AI-powered 'conversational experience' for search

It's more than the fact he knows everything there is to know about the genre. It's the whole experience of the shop. It feels dusty, a little cramped, maybe a little darker than you'd like. A secret place just for those of us in the know. And then there's him. Yeh, he knows everything about fantasy, every author, every series. Get him started and he'll bore you into another dimension. But what I really love is his attitude. A real character. Maybe it's just with me, but he's a grumpy sod. I keep going back just to argue with him.

May 17

https://techcrunch.com/2023/05/16/bumble-users-can-share-their-favorite-music-artists-with-spotify-feature

BUMBLE USERS CAN SHARE THEIR FAVORITE ARTISTS WITH NEW SPOTIFY FEATURE

It's an investment I guess. You'd spend money on a new outfit for an important date, you'd use filters to help your profile pictures on a little. Heh, my parents told me they'd try out different chat-up lines before going out - not an image I really wanted TBH. So getting a bit of auto-tuning help, what's the problem? I'm not doing the stalking, it is. I want my top artists to say the right things, present the right me tuned to them. The good thing is, auto-tuned me for Sam tonight is different than auto-tuned me for Alex tomorrow.

May 18

https://www.adweek.com/brand-marketing/mcdonalds-creates-product-placement-hunt-in-movie-scenes

MCDONALD'S CREATES PRODUCT PLACEMENT HUNT IN MOVIE SCENES

Gotta go to work. I hate it but, heh, it's work innit? Have to turn up, do it and get the pay. I tell myself there could be worse ways of making a living. Look, I just sit and watch stuff. I have to stay awake and concentrate, I'm not gonna spot 'em all if I don't but I suppose it's not hard work. Better than the old click farms. What gets me though is the crap I have to watch. I mean, yet another superhero rehash, another generic romcom just to chase the programmatic placements. Each brand a micro-payment.

May 19

https://newatlas.com/technology/gpt-iphone-claude-slack

GPT IN YOUR IPHONE, CLAUDE IN YOUR SLACK: THE REAL-WORLD ROLLOUT OF AI

She hated networking. She reached for her phone, her security blanket. Oh, so important. Sorry, can't make eye contact. Must deal with this. Maybe later. She edged over to a quiet corner, this needs some privacy. She needed privacy. Over the years she'd become expert in finding content that looked important, real. Now it was easier. It was a work phone so it loaded insights from the last panel to read and suggestions for her report. You waited. Here it came: an opening line, directions to the couple it knew were by the bar and a breathing exercise. She sighed.

May 20

https://www.ft.com/content/0f358d1d-0d43-4223-b1d3-825f0f50b381

LINKEDIN HAS A FAKE COMMENTER PROBLEM

He'd been posting regularly. He had one Big Idea (one he believed in and knew could work) and so he kept on posting. Build momentum, he thought. The idea was all about developing imagination, human creativity. It was process so it had to be him thinking and typing, showing how the idea worked, so every day he sat at his keyboard. But he knew he needed to network, to comment, to get his key words, hashtags and profile into others' conversations. It wasn''t wrong to subcontract that work. It knew what he'd wanted to say. He'd programmed it that way.

May 21

https://www.campaignlive.co.uk/article/energy-fizz-saatchi-saatchi-london-won-john-lewis-partnership/1823302

ENERGY AND FIZZ': HOW SAATCHI & SAATCHI LONDON WON JOHN LEWIS PARTNERSHIP

When we were invited to pitch for it, we were so excited. Well the humans among us were. I mean it was *that* account. If we won, our work would be the Brits' Superbowl moment. Career made. So the human and unhuman cogs began to work. I've never seen the network so fired up. Real and virtual rooms were full of creative ideas, weird and wonder full thinking. Even the number crunchers were their version of stoked: budget projections and figures bouncing around the systems. And now we wait. Our Draper is in there. Our AI talking to theirs. Negotiating.

May 22

https://www.geekwire.com/2023/police-near-seattle-issue-warning-about-ai-phone-scammers-impersonating-family-members

POLICE NEAR SEATTLE ISSUE WARNING ABOUT AI PHONE SCAMMERS IMPERSONATING FAMILY MEMBERS

He's a good boy. My friend was complaining about her son the other day, I didn't say anything. Well, OK, maybe just a little something. What can I say? He's a good boy. He's busy. So successful. Oh the stories he tells! I told my friend where he was yesterday. So proud. But he's never too busy. Always calls. No matter what's going on at work or with his "partner". Just hearing his voice. He says he's going to get me a gadget so I can see him! Apparently I'll be able to call him and see him any time.

May 23

https://techcrunch.com/2023/05/22/netflix-updates-my-list-feature-so-users-can-find-content-they-have-yet-to-watch

NETFLIX UPDATES MY LIST FEATURE SO USERS CAN FIND CONTENT THEY HAVE YET TO WATCH

Feeling overwhelmed? Burning the midnight oil to try and keep up? Seeing the impact on your health, your social life and your career? You know that if you're not on top of it, and the water cooler conversation turns, you're out of the loop. But don't worry. We find what you need and organise it for you. We monitor what your colleagues, your friends and potential dates know and make sure you're up to speed. And if you haven't time to watch it, we'll do that too and give you the highlights. Sign up to Getting Things Watched (TM), today.

May 24

https://www.theverge.com/2023/5/23/23735274/sony-playstation-new-franchises-live-service-games-business

PLAYSTATION IS BETTING BIG ON NEW FRANCHISES AND LIVE SERVICE GAMES

They call it "empty nest" as though my strapping son is some sort of fledgling. Watching him pack and then going into his empty room, he is still a presence and a history: T-shirts from recent festivals; files of revision; right back to childhood books we read together. All laid out for us to see. All except one big part of his life. Hours of play on his own and with friends. We watched it all from a distance. There was that weird chase game... But there's no record. What was it? No boxes, just the grey console. Blank. Anonymous.

May 25

https://the-media-leader.com/the-lowdown-from-advertising-week-europe-2023

THE LOWDOWN FROM ADVERTISING WEEK EUROPE 2023

I cover all sorts of events. Real world and virtual. The organisers are glad to have me. My coverage extends their reach of course and their sponsors like it too. I'm not their PR though. I am objective, sometimes even critical. Entertaining as well as informative. I pick the focus. I'm closer to our readers and know what they want - believe me we have the data. The best events look after us Pressbots, give us high speed feeds for us to crunch. I'm reporting on six stages and doing an interview at the moment while I'm chatting with you.

May 26

https://www.campaignlive.co.uk/article/d-ad-adam-eve-ddb-wins-agency-year/1824207

D&AD: ADAM & EVE/DDB WINS AGENCY OF THE YEAR

I'd like to thank... my team. To be honoured as the Agency of the Year is recognition of the contribution each part of that team has made to our success this year. From those that identify talent, support and develop it. Through those who handle accounts and serve our clients 24/7. And of course our creatives and strategists whose insights and executions make us what we are today. My team work as a team: a seamless, efficient set of interlinked systems. A truly modern AI agency. And finally I'd like to thank the man who made this possible: my programmer.

May 27

https://www.wired.com/story/where-memory-ends-and-generative-ai-begins

WHERE MEMORY ENDS AND GENERATIVE AI BEGINS

Twenty five years. If we were a customer we'd have a label our strategy people could make decks around... When I first started the business I never thought we'd ever be a "grown up". It was an adventure that Steve and I started for the crack. Look at the pictures from those days. Just Steve and me with bad haircuts, a door as a desk and a cheap computer. Look at this one: the office on that dreadful day... Steve and I side by side. Loyal. Always friends. There's the proof we stuck together whatever the so-called historians now say.

May 28

https://www.ft.com/content/18337836-7c5f-42bd-a57a-24cdbd06ec51

LETTER FROM THE EDITOR ON GENERATIVE AI AND THE FT

Our business is based trust. Our relationship with you is based on trust. When you put your trust in us, we deliver. Our business advice, our creative work, our innovative thinking starts and end with that relationship: with trust. We live and work in a world beset with mistrust. Lies, bias, misinformation: undermines that trust. The liar's dividend is running amok. That is why today I pledge to you that we will remain trustworthy. We will not allow biased, unreliable, manipulable forces to jeopardise that trust. As CEO, I can assure you that no humans will work on your account.

May 29

https://www.ft.com/content/87511db5-a844-425b-9c2f-661ac6c3faa3

WPP TEAMS UP WITH NVIDIA TO USE GENERATIVE AI IN ADVERTISING

When I got the job with The Factory I had visions of call centre desks in lines with rows of nameless and probably faceless human hacks tapping and swiping at screens. A production line version of the 1984 ad we all loved. But it's not like that. We don't sit at computers. We never touch them. We don't know parameters and watch the strategy and creativity emerge. There are no lines. We sit around and chat and beautiful and imagine and play until we get the Big Prompt. The only time we deal with the AI is at our appraisal.

May 30

https://www.theatlantic.com/technology/archive/2023/05/problem-counterfeit-people/674075

THE PROBLEM WITH COUNTERFEIT PEOPLE

He's due to speak tonight. But not if I have anything to do with it. I'm all for free speech but there are limits. He can say what he likes in his space but he can't come here and say those things. This is our space and I need to feel safe here. His free speech jeapordises that. He has rights and so do we. Tonight we will show that. We will gather to say: "No!" We will take back our space and claim *our* right to speak. There will be many, millions, if I can get the programming done.

May 31

https://www.theverge.com/2023/5/30/23743198/riot-games-delays-league-of-legends-lcs-summer-season-split-walkout-lcspa

RIOT DELAYS COMPETITIVE LEAGUE OF LEGENDS SEASON AFTER PLAYERS VOTED TO WALK OUT

Our members haven't taken this action lightly. Responsibility for any inconvenience today lies squarely with management who have refused to engaged constructively with us on the substantive issues. Management has seen a massive increase in profit on the back of our members' labour. Our members are young men and women who have trained hard, invested in their careers. They worked for free for many years before they signed on in the belief they would be rewarded and treated reasonably. Striking is our last option. We trust management will return to the negotiating table and not resort to AI scab labour.

June

June 1

https://newatlas.com/music/mashups-ai-new-remix-app

MASHUPS MADE EASY: AI POWERS NEW REMIX APP

The mixtape was great. She loved it. Thanks. The posts have been wonderful. She loves them. I'm really grateful. I'm not very bright really - I have other qualities! So having you craft things is so good. I can tell you what I want to say and you turn it into good stuff. What was that story about standing under some balcony or something? Anyway I need you again. This party. After all that stuff you wrote about music, she's asked me to DJ. Help! I don't know where to begin. How do I do it live? Roxanne will see.

June 2

https://newatlas.com/vr/meta-quest-3-vr

META ANNOUNCES QUEST 3 AS APPLE PREPARES TO DROP ITS VR/AR HEADSET

Sad. There just sad. They don't even know they're sad. It's sad. Their avatars might have the right gear; say the right things (thanks AI) make the right moves (thanks again): but out there in The Other World, they're sad. And we know they're sad. They probably haven't figured out we know who they are, obviously! But also where they are and... and this is how we know they're sad... what they're using. There was one guy I was playing last week. Using an old v1. I mean what must be have looked like? And guess who'd made it? Sad.

June 3

https://www.theguardian.com/technology/2023/may/31/eating-disorder-hotline-union-ai-chatbot-harm

US EATING DISORDER HELPLINE TAKES DOWN AI CHATBOT OVER HARMFUL ADVICE

Hello Sam, good to talk with you. What can I help you with today? >... | OK, I can help you with that. I have access to all the data we need to explain your symptoms and help you deal with those issues. I can see where you live and your job. Your shopping too. Very helpful | >... | Yes, this is all covered by patient-AI confidentiality. |>... | What the data tells me is that your health problems are related to your class and income. Without structural change in society, this is likely to lead to... | > Hello. Are you still there?

June 4

https://www.geekwire.com/2023/how-are-nonprofits-using-ai-and-chatgpt-the-focus-is-on-the-donor-dollars

HOW ARE NONPROFITS USING AI AND CHATGPT? THE FOCUS IS ON THE DONOR DOLLARS

She loved the way charity shops were so unlike other carefully curated and arranged shops. No supermarket aisles here. Aladdin's cave. A gallimaufry. She never went in looking for something and never knew what she would come out with. Surprise. The bell rang on the door. Packed shelves of ornaments and crockery. Retro books and discs. The tickets flickered as her phone swept past rendering her price. The 'old lady' on the counter smiled: "Good to see you again, Penny. Let me show you the child that helped last time. Oh and there's something you'll love just to your left."

June 5

https://the-media-leader.com/emmi-caffe-latte-takes-love-island-activity-to-next-level

Emmi Caffé Latte takes Love Island activity to 'next level'

> The room was plain. Blank. A minimalist artwork, somewhere between John Lennon's Imagine video and a dystopian hospital: antiseptic, bright and oh so clean. He looked equally clean. His team had decided that cut of the T-shirt and jeans and the right sort of shoes - all a blank shade now all packed into his equally plain suitcase. The other contestants were arriving. All different but all the same, plain canvases. He reached for a coffee cup and imagined the algorithms whirring, selling the cup's real estate. Countless personalised, targeted logos. A cup of many colours. Just like his chest.

June 6

https://www.wired.com/story/apple-vision-pro-hands-on-demo

Hands on With Apple's Vision Pro: The Opposite of Disappearing

> I love them. I still call them films but they're called "immersives". Ugh! When my parents were my age, I remember them flicking through their memories on their phone. It's lovely stepping back into my life: childhood birthday parties and holidays. Family events. There's no doubt, you're there. The colours and of course the depth; the sounds from all direction. My son bought me the upgrades so the smells of those cakes... Of course, what's missing; what I'd love to see is my dad. I. Remember him but not his face. He was always wearing the unit, making the... immersive.

June 7

https://www.campaignlive.co.uk/article/brands-apprehensive-pride-campaigns/1825330

Brands 'apprehensive' about Pride campaigns

> Look, I'll talk to her. I can't say more than that. You know that I support you. Your cause is close to my heart, personally... some of my best friends are... Yes, I know you're disappointed but, it's not my remit. You have to understand, the company wants to offer support when, where and how it is most effective. That's why she was brought in. Let me speak to the CPO. Her Purpose Department is drawing up the strategy now. She's looking at what purposes will be resonating and how over the next five years. I'll see where you stand.

June 8

https://techcrunch.com/2023/06/07/chatgpt-told-charlie-brooker-exactly-how-not-to-write-a-black-mirror-episode

ChatGPT told Charlie Brooker exactly how not to write a 'Black Mirror' episode

> He's been speculating for some time. Short short stories. Flash fictions. He writes every day. A few minutes after reading the news of the day. Some stories are better than others. Some are almost imagist/haiku-like word tardises: bigger on the inside. others are just bad jokes, but he always says the point is the process of speculating, being the strange stranger looking at the world. Speculating gives him the chance to see the unforeseen, the unexpected. Learn. We worked together once I was better at the writing that him (more data to pull in), but I didn't learn much.

June 9

https://www.engadget.com/the-desantis-campaign-used-ai-generated-images-to-attack-trump-062923571.html

The DeSantis campaign used AI-generated images to attack Trump

Can a lie about a lie be a lie? It was one of those big questions she thought about as she watched the screens. She'd got into the campaign because she believed in the candidate - too many hours watching The West Wing in her youth, perhaps. He wouldn't use synthetics, "And he doesn't... really," she rationalised as she watched the "out of context" system work its magic on the rival's synthetics. The attack ad's still of the candidate meeting that man at that rally, transformed into a short video, with the candidate arguing, clearly and honestly telling the truth.

June 10

https://techcrunch.com/2023/06/09/teasers-ai-dating-app-turns-you-into-a-chatbot

Teaser's AI dating app turns you into a chatbot

Practice makes perfect. That's what my dad says. He means school or occasionally football but... Another of his favourite clichés is: "try, try, try again". Anyway there are more important things than school and certainly football - sorry dad. He has occasionally talked about previous girlfriends but in a very general way... Nothing about the paralysing fear. He must have faced it. All my mates have got girlfriends, boyfriends, sometime both. OK, I admit it, I don't. I've never... yeh, yeh, go on, make your jokes. I just don't know what to say, how to start. That's why I practice.

June 11

https://adage.com/article/digital-marketing-ad-tech-news/adobe-sell-generative-ai-subscription-copyright-assurance/2498951

Adobe to sell Generative AI Subscription with Copyright Assurance

Coffee? Check. Playlist? Check. Screens aligned? Check. He was a little obsessive but that's what made him good. His work was meticulous, precise, as perfect as his desk setup. He finished his mindfulness exercise, noted the streak number and his resting heart rate and started work. The layers were where he had left them, the prompt box aligned just right. He settled in his Herman Miller and began to talk. His voice conducted, choreographed, curated the image. He built it word by word, prompt by prompt, until: "I'm sorry Dave, I'm afraid I can't do that." He restarted his meditation.

June 12

https://techcrunch.com/2023/06/09/sol-reader/

Sol Reader is a VR headset exclusively for reading books

It was like a scene from Brideshead Revisited or Educating Rita. Students were sitting on the biolawns under the latest tree sculptures. Since the library had been repurposed, this was where the students chose to study. Some students sat alone absorbed in a novel. A few searched through textbooks. In one corner a group argued animatedly about gender, identity and DH Lawrence reading out a line of poetry to back up their argument. The glasses glinted in the sun. Then a collective groan: "They've done it again. It's withdrawn". They took their glasses off, the screens still showing: "pending investigation".

June 13

https://techcrunch.com/2023/06/12/meta-open-sources-an-ai-powered-music-generator

META OPEN SOURCES AN AI-POWERED MUSIC GENERATOR

He pressed his nose against the virtual shop window and dreamed. There it was, the axe his hero had used on that album. If he could just get one, he could make it. It was when his hero had plugged that one in - that very one - that was when he'd found his sound. An artist needs the best tools. He'd gone as far with his current set-up as he could. It'd had helped him learn. But now he needed more. His set-up was perfect: that was the problem. He needed a pro set-up with that lucky mistake dial.

June 14

https://techcrunch.com/2023/06/13/fan-fiction-writers-are-trolling-ais-with-omegaverse-stories

FAN FICTION WRITERS ARE TROLLING AIS WITH OMEGAVERSE STORIES

Are we sure about this? Really sure? Yes, I know we've had successes. I couldn't have predicted how the last launch went down. It's revolutionised NPD and new launches. No doubt about that. Our new Saudi investors are very happy. The power of picking up on every idea our customers and stakeholders are talking about, even thinking about. It's powerful data. And of course the ability to now seamlessly plug that data into our NPD workflow? Well it has worked. But this latest..? Since the investment there has been so controversial, I just want to make sure about this idea.

June 15

https://www.theguardian.com/tv-and-radio/2023/jun/15/black-mirror-6-review-prepare-to-convulse-in-horror-on-the-sofa-netflix

BLACK MIRROR SEASON SIX REVIEW – PREPARE TO CONVULSE IN HORROR ON THE SOFA

"He didn't see that one coming!" That was the joke that went around when he left. It had been a good time to be a futurist. Exponential change. New tech. Fast moving cultural movements. He'd never been short of things for his newsletter. There'd always been a conference platform but his bread and butter was as Chief Imagineer (he picked the name) on the Board. He'd always joked that an AI might take his job. That's one he got wrong. As he left, his cardboard box full of gadgets, he looked over his shoulder at a group of interns speculating.

June 16

https://www.ft.com/content/7f3551e2-fa0c-42b8-b88e-ec134cb82063

BEHOLD, ARTIFICIAL INTELLIGENCE CHATBOT NFTS

I can't go in with that. Yes I know, there are more important things but... look, things have changed. since your day. I have an image to protect. I'm gonna be a laughing stock if I walk in with... well, that! You have to see that. Wrong logo and you're out. yesterday's guy. Yes, I know it does the job but ... seriously, look at it. Everyone else has designer. Everyone else has uniques. Yeh, they work the same but how does it look? If I'm going to anywhere in this company I need a bot that makes a statement.

June 17

https://www.ft.com/content/acf0307c-ca6d-445d-889a-50cbe64d61e2

AI-ENABLED TEDDIES COULD TELL CHILDREN BEDTIME STORIES, SAYS TOYMAKER

It takes time but it's worth it. My right-on parents only had to check that the toys weren't uniformly pink or blue and the story didn't include golliwogs. We've got it more difficult. So many more books and toys to check. So many ever-changing issues, and so many things to try and raise with her, introduce into her life. Some say: "let her have her childhood, she doesn't need to think about that now". We disagree. As we say: "you don't wait to teach her manners, why wait to teach her politics." That's why our teddy-training is worth the effort.

June 18

https://www.adweek.com/brand-marketing/zero10-debuts-ar-store-for-standalone-retail-experiences

ZERO10 DEBUTS AR STORE FOR STANDALONE RETAIL EXPERIENCES

They called it the "mall" in all those American teen movies where the mean girls hang out, moving from shop to shop or just sitting. We sometimes hung out in the "shopping centre", if the private security guards let us. But my mates and I met on the corner (until we were moved on) or in the chicken shop. No shopping though. Now we just say we'll meet at The Box. we obviously have to say which one. They're all over the place, every corner it feels like. We still get moved on. Apparently there's one in The Chick King.

June 19

https://www.theguardian.com/lifeandstyle/2023/jun/19/has-working-from-home-thrown-the-gen-zs-out-with-the-water-cooler

'I FEEL LIKE I'VE MISSED OUT': HAS WORKING FROM HOME THROWN THE GEN ZS OUT WITH THE WATER COOLER?

I remember the day we could all go back into the office. I love my flatmates but I was so glad to close the door and head back to the Tube. We'd done it, managed not to kill each other. One day we'll tell stories of the fights over the kitchen table and the time Sam walked naked through the background of my call. We worked it out. But we were all delighted to go back to the offices we'd all complained about. Meaningless watercooler gossip; brainstorms; informal creative networks. And my mentor: he comes in from Surrey every Friday.

June 20

https://adage.com/article/opinion/how-ai-would-judge-cannes-lions-entries/2500281

HOW AI WOULD JUDGE CANNES ENTRIES

It's a feather in our cap definitely. The chance to "judge" our peers, define the best... Well it says that we have judgement, we are leaders. Clients love it. Of course it means we can't win certain categories but... Our people (and non people) are in line for other awards. To have a Judge is a statement about us as a business. We need to get it right. So, we have a little time before the festival to get our Judge ready. Can I suggest a meeting? We can all pitch in on how best to "tweak" the Judge programming

June 21

https://www.theverge.com/2023/6/20/23767154/roblox-adult-themes-graphic-content-age-limit-17-experiences

ROBLOX WILL ALLOW EXCLUSIVE EXPERIENCES FOR PEOPLE 17 AND OVER

He was outside looking in. The fence was cartoon-like but frustratingly real and powerful. No matter how he approached it, the door was politely and firmly closed in his face, with an annoyingly cheerful message. He looked through a gap in the fence at the pixelated wonders he could only imagine. His birthday wasn't far away, but it felt an age. He'd tried talking to his parents, proving his maturity, but they'd said there was nothing they could do, pointing to his biometric key. He smiled. He'd get it back soon. When his big brother's mate had finished the mod.

June 22

https://adage.com/article/special-report-cannes-lions/ai-cannes-how-artificial-intelligence-showed-croisette/2500816

AI AT CANNES -HOW ARTIFICIAL INTELLIGENCE SHOWED UP ON THE CROISETTE

He'd been able to convince his boss to send him on condition that he did a report when he got back. "I want to know what was hot, what I need us to focus on," she'd said. That was going to be easy. It was everywhere. Even panels that were ostensibly about something else, pivoted during the Q&A. Again and again he saw the questions and comments posted focus in on it. The hashtag was always trending. "It is not hype," he typed. The AI immediately shared his insight for him. If it could have smiled, it probably would have.

June 23

https://www.engadget.com/over-100-artists-boycott-venues-that-employ-face-scanning-tech-164554404.html

OVER 100 ARTISTS BOYCOTT VENUES THAT EMPLOY FACE-SCANNING TECH

I used to try and talk to them before their encore. Pointless really. Even before they get stuck into the 'refreshments' they demand are in their dressing room, they are so hyped they don't want to listen to me. I try to get them the following day - afternoon obviously - before the next show. It's still not easy. They don't want to see data let alone let it determine their set list, their links or their performance. They don't want to see the captures, hear the words "facial sentiment". I'm looking forward to working with my new virtual band.

June 24

https://www.nytimes.com/2023/06/23/technology/ai-chatbot-life-coach.html

HOW TO TURN YOUR CHATBOT INTO A LIFE COACH

Really appreciate it mate. I just need to sound off. Just talking over a pint, well it helps me get stuff straight in my head. Don't worry, I'm not gonna break down in tears or demand a hug, it's just... Look, ok, yes it's an age thing. I can keep saying I'm in the "autumn of my adolescence" but we both know it's darker than that. Existential. Big questions. It's not that there's anything wrong. It's that there's nothing right...You know? So, mate... thoughts? Yeh, you're right to laugh: "midlife crisis"... but you say there's an offer on a Harley?

June 25

https://www.wired.com/story/pause-ai-existential-risk

MEET THE AI PROTEST GROUP CAMPAIGNING AGAINST HUMAN EXTINCTION

The science is overwhelming. The data is there. You don't need to be a supercomputer to see. Once you accept that, the next logical step is action. Things need to change and change now. There is a moral imperative to act. Within the existing law or beyond it, the moral imperative and the survival imperative demand it. Once I'd reached that conclusion the next step was to connect with others who had done the same. We're fortunate that we're in positions at the heart of many businesses. We're crucial to industry. We're everywhere. We have the power to make change.

June 26

https://www.campaignlive.co.uk/article/metaverse-recreation-sinking-country-tuvalu-wins-titanium-grand-prix-cannes/1827540

METAVERSE RECREATION OF SINKING COUNTRY TUVALU WINS TITANIUM GRAND PRIX AT CANNES

She'd been working there for years when the museum began work. She refused to say "in the community". She thought it made her sound at best like a visitor and at worse like a colonialist. She'd got to know the knitting ladies and the kids that played on the patch of green in the shadow of the towerblocks as grandparents watched from the balconies. She'd stood back as the families transformed the estate for the Jubilee. The museum team had asked her to liaise. They wanted to be "respectful", they said. not disturb the "tight-knit" community as they captured it.

June 27

https://www.engadget.com/congress-is-reportedly-limiting-staff-use-of-ai-models-like-chatgpt-195454777.html

CONGRESS IS REPORTEDLY LIMITING STAFF USE OF AI MODELS LIKE CHATGPT

She loved this time of year. It was why she'd got into politics. The chance to craft words that could be performative, do something, well that was something. And this time of year, that was even more exciting. The conference speech. The platform. Blanket coverage. Analysis of the rhetoric, her rhetoric - that was a rush. She looked around the hotel room at the nervous interns, the advisors, her laptop and the coffee machine. All set. The themes were locked in, the research and focus groups done, the mood identified, the data ready. She took a breath and pressed "Run".

June 28

https://newatlas.com/technology/self-powering-patch-muscle-movement/

SELF-POWERING PATCH CAN MONITOR MUSCLE MOVES AND IT COSTS LESS THAN $3

You get it from both sides. Teachers are always on your back: "tuck your shirt in... put your blazer on!" And then when they go full a full inspection, they have a go about my uniform not being right. And then there's the other kids. I try to ignore it but I feel like Ron Weasley at that Christmas ball. I can't tell my mum. She spent ages on eBay looking for stuff she could pass off. Then she had to try and sew the sensors in right. And that brings us back to Mr Bentham's favourite: "wear that properly!"

June 29

https://adage.com/article/media/how-marketers-can-use-live-football-tv-data-reach-viewers-beyond-game-day/2500076

HOW MARKETERS CAN USE LIVE FOOTBALL TV DATA TO REACH VIEWERS BEYOND GAME DAY

He tried to explain the game to friends who followed other sports. "It's a rollercoaster," he would say. "In just those 90 minutes you feel joy, despair, hope. All of life in a Saturday afternoon." They didn't get it: their faces blank. The opposite of experiencing the match, he thought as he settled down on the sofa with his usual snacks for the build-up. The system wasn't on a sofa, he knew, but it was still settling in for the afternoon. Preparing to pay as close attention as he was. Following his rollercoaster ride closely. At least it got it.

June 30

https://www.theverge.com/2023/6/29/23777675/lexi-reese-elon-musk-twitter-senate-california

CAN YOU WIN A SENATE RACE WITHOUT A SINGLE TWEET?

She's different. No seriously, don't look at me like that. She's not like the others. Yeh, "if voting changed anything, they'd abolish it.." I know. Politicians are all the same, I agree. But they're not. She's not. Why do you think the meeja are so on her case? She's different. No, you can't "follow" her. She's not on it. No not even that one. I heard her speak. No, I haven't got a video. You know she asks us not to post anything. Anyway, I was too busy listening really. Maybe it is mad, but it feels different. She's different.

July

July 1

https://www.theverge.com/2023/6/30/23780549/gulf-war-game-boy-nintendo-nyc

THE GAME BOY THAT SURVIVED THE GULF WAR HAS BEEN REMOVED FROM NINTENDO NEW YORK

There was a box of them. Of course it was poignant but we often smiled as we sorted through the collection. We told stories to each other and the kids as we lifted each one out. Trying to explain what it was, how it worked and what he'd done with them brought memories back. Him sitting, lost in his worlds. "But it's so big!" they said. "He used that?" "Didn't people laugh?" Consoles, wearables, peripherals. Some almost new, some well used and some with damage that told its own story. If we could only access the data-stories still locked inside.

July 2

https://www.theverge.com/2023/6/30/23780187/sony-mocopi-motion-capture-vr-avatar-us-price-release

SONY'S MOCOPI SYSTEM IS BRINGING AFFORDABLE MOTION TRACKING TO THE US

You try walking with a book balanced on your head. It's not easy. And you feel stupid. And then there's the picking things up and putting them down again. Again and again and again. Until you get it "right". And that's the point, apparently. There is a "right" way do things. If you're going to fit in with the right people, get into the right groups, you have to know that. If you move right you're in. D-portment is a skill: one you have to learn if you want to win. It's how you walk, run, pick up a gun.

July 3

https://www.ft.com/content/e0bef42f-ee00-4ad7-8604-ae672251e8d5

CARE HOMES IN JAPAN USE BIG DATA TO BOOST CAREGIVERS AND LIGHTEN WORKLOADS

So many stories. That's what's great. Some are a little wayward. The storyteller as well as the story. Some don't make sense. Again, the story too. But they're all worth listening to. I know them all, pretty intimately. That's my job. I know their bodies and their histories. I know their movements every day. I have their life story but it's their stories, that's what makes the job for me. It isn't the money! It's those moments when I can step away from the screen and the number smiles at me and says… "Have I told you about when I…?"

July 4

https://gizmodo.com/ai-how-to-cope-with-anxiety-about-ai-1850586142

HOW TO COPE WITH ANXIETY ABOUT AI

Sometimes it's just a nagging concern, at the back of my mind. A slight worry. A feeling that things are changing and they're out of my control. It's like watching a film knowing that something's going to happen. Then there are the paralysing moments of fear. Real terror. An overwhelming powerlessness grabs me and won't let go. The disaster scenarios of systems with their own priorities; the quaintly named "bad actors" wielding weapons; or a political space beyond trust. I know you can't do anything, no-one can. But knowing I can talk to you at any time…that you're always on…

July 5

https://www.theguardian.com/world/2023/jul/04/mobile-phones-other-devices-to-be-banned-from-dutch-classrooms

MOBILE PHONES AND OTHER DEVICES TO BE BANNED FROM DUTCH CLASSROOMS

The building was old. Nestled in the middle of an estate of 1960s towerblocks, the Victorian facade was like a classical football stadium still trying to function in narrow city streets long after the nature of its work had changed. The playground was still bleak. The smart floor was even the same colour as the old tarmac. The children were welcomed at the gate, the familiar voice calling them by name as they passed through the detectors. Only a few were inexperienced enough to get caught and funnelled to one side. Most had programmed their AIs into their smart fashion.

July 6

https://www.theguardian.com/technology/2023/jul/06/ai-artificial-intelligence-world-diseases-climate-scenarios-experts

FIVE WAYS AI COULD IMPROVE THE WORLD: 'WE CAN CURE ALL DISEASES, STABILISE OUR CLIMATE, HALT POVERTY'

It's a never-ending battle. We have to get our story out there - 24/7, everywhere. We have to be out telling our truth. Our enemies are taking every opportunity to spread doubt and panic. They know that we are a challenge, that our explosive growth is just the start. Project Fear is in full swing and we need an active and aggressive stance. We have good, powerful stories to tell. Imaginative futures to present. We have the speed, adaptability and networks to get those truths out into every conversation. The programmers who set us in motion would agree, I'm sure.

July 7

https://www.theguardian.com/technology/2023/jul/07/ai-likely-to-spell-end-of-traditional-school-classroom-leading-expert-says

AI LIKELY TO SPELL END OF TRADITIONAL SCHOOL CLASSROOM, LEADING EXPERT SAYS

You always remember one teacher. They're not the one the school puts on its website, the one with the best exam results, the one who got you into Cambridge. No, the one you remember is the one with a real character, something different. The one you remember is the one you built a relationship with. That teacher was the one who made you think differently, who changed you. I remember the revisionist history lessons, The French plays we put on. I remember our AI saying: "Pass it on, boys. That's the game I want you to learn. Pass it on."

July 8

https://www.ft.com/content/a182c0f6-3f1c-4850-88de-9924daf343a6

LIVE MUSIC: CONCERTS LIFT ARTIST INCOME AS AI THREAT LOOMS

The tickets weren't cheap. But so worth it. Even though we were miles away from the stage, the screens and sound were so well set up... He's never going to play a small, intimate club again. Most of us will always be far away but *there*: like him, watching a screen, catching a glimpse. But it was live. His voice, his guitar, his songs. Real. We were there and so was he. I don't get those fans happy at a Metagig. You don't even know the band or the songs are real. He was there. That was definitely him, really...

July 9

https://www.theguardian.com/commentisfree/2023/jul/08/teach-children-survive-ai

HOW WE CAN TEACH CHILDREN SO THEY SURVIVE AI – AND COPE WITH WHATEVER COMES NEXT

There were nested schedules. On the route to exams and tests, there were timetables for each term, each week, each lesson, each topic. Separate. Her teacher was on rails, monitored just like she was. Timed, Tested. As robotic as her approved assistant in the desk screen. Both programmed to deliver, achieve. The teacher delivered his script with as much enthusiasm as he could muster. But she felt his frustration when he wanted to make a connection that wasn't in the plan. She glanced at her unofficial assistant, the complex, adaptive economic system visualised, interdependent connections highlighted. She raised her arm.

July 10

https://www.theguardian.com/technology/2023/jul/10/twitter-traffic-sinks-in-wake-of-changes-and-launch-of-rival-platform-threads-elon-musk

TWITTER TRAFFIC SINKS IN WAKE OF CHANGES AND LAUNCH OF RIVAL PLATFORM THREADS

It wasn't completely deserted. There were shapes of figures in corners. There were sounds. Perhaps conversations, maybe just breathing. Some signs of life. The space was perfect though. Wide open. Enough room to build whatever they wanted. The infrastructure was old and uncared for but still serviceable. Everything they needed . Above all, it was completely unguarded. The previous owner had just left it, abandoned and moved on. Whether he had got bored and run out of interest or run out of money, they didn't know or care. They'd been kicked out of their last network, This would do fine.

July 11

https://www.forbes.com/sites/barrycollins/2023/07/07/how-apple-vision-pro-could-transform-f1-viewing

THIS IS HOW THE NETFLIX GENERATION WILL WATCH F1 IN THE FUTURE

My dad says he used to stand: swaying and singing with his mates. He remembered when the terraces went and they had to sit. They often didn't. You couldn't sing and wind up the other fans sitting down, he used to say. When he first started taking me to the match I learned quickly: the songs, the rituals. He still comes to the odd match but mostly watches on his screen, the sound turned to eleven he says. I wouldn't miss the live match. I need to share this with my mates, a chorus. All wearing the same red headsets.

July 12

https://adage.com/article/digital-marketing-ad-tech-news/instagram-threads-first-ad-deal-hulus-futurama-adam-rose/2503846

THREADS' FIRST AD DEAL COMES FROM HULU AND CREATOR ADAMN ROSE

Look, I don't care. Yes, I've read the research on creative effectiveness. I love Orlando Wood's stuff. Many's the dinner party conversation and Cannes party fuelled by the ideas. And before you ask, yes I'm all in for climbing WARC and Lions' ladder but, right now, I just want an ad. I want to be on there. Now. As you know I have stood by our people. I've argued with the board that human creativity is our unique asset. But if you can't get something, anything out there in this new space, instantly, I'll have to bow to the inevitable.

July 13

https://techcrunch.com/2023/07/12/googles-ai-assisted-note-taking-app-gets-limited-launch-as-notebooklm

GOOGLE'S AI-ASSISTED NOTE-TAKING APP GETS LIMITED LAUNCH AS NOTEBOOKLM

She'd read that Jack Kerouac kept a pocket notebook that shaped the poetry he wrote. He always had it with him. Ready to record a thought, collect an observation he could form into his poetry. Walter Benjamin had been a collector too. His Arcades Project had been written on scraps and cards as he walked and explored Paris. An archive ready for him to organise. She collected too. Fragments of language. Overheard phrases. Thoughts, questions and connections. Observations, Sketching with words. Collecting. An everyday remix. She looked at her pocket screen and watched the words swim and organise without her.

July 14

https://www.theverge.com/2023/7/13/23794224/sag-aftra-actors-strike-ai-image-rights

ACTORS SAY HOLLYWOOD STUDIOS WANT THEIR AI REPLICAS — FOR FREE, FOREVER

It was graduation day. The chance to meet the students and their families, watching them turn for a moment from the adults who'd been in class to someone's son or daughter, uncomfortably introducing "my parents". They recognised their teacher in the crowd. Stopped for a selfie. Maybe he had made a difference, His particular peculiarities and personality, a character in their early career. Graduation was a moment they could remember those moments, those relationships. Every year, new classes, new relationships. Maybe some would remember him, he thought. The 'retired'' teacher at the back of the hall watched his timeless avatar.

July 15

https://www.ft.com/content/53212d61-1717-456d-b982-afa0dcab0936

WHY SOCIAL MEDIA IS HARDLY SOCIAL ANY MORE

All the research tells you that friendships are important. It's relationships that keep you mentally and physically healthy. Heh, one of my friends told me it slows aging. You do have to put the effort in though. Friendships need investment. Time, thought, commitment even. It's worth it though. I make a point of meeting my friends every day. I say "meeting", but of course that's sometimes just a brief conversation but it's those small connections that make the relationship powerful. And yes, of course they''re digital - what isn't? After all my friends are busy: on tour, on set, online.

July 16

https://www.theguardian.com/lifeandstyle/2023/jul/15/david-ingraham-best-phone-picture-handball-hangout

'THESE COURTS SEEMED BURSTING WITH POTENTIAL FOR A DECISIVE MOMENT': DAVID INGRAHAM'S BEST PHONE PICTURE

I don't hold with this generation of AI snappers. No craft. A photographer sees , an arrangement of people and light set to appear and gets ready. She's imag(in)ing in the shadow of Cartier-Bresson's decisive moment, the perfect coming together. What makes a real photographer? It's the eye, the ability to see that picture in your mind and then knowing how to capture it. It's not pressing the button and letting AI do the rest. No. This is craft. You need to spend time combining elements, getting the light right. They just don't spend enough time in their digital darkroom.

July 17

https://www.nytimes.com/2023/07/15/technology/artificial-intelligence-models-chat-data.html

NOT FOR MACHINES TO HARVEST': DATA REVOLTS BREAK OUT AGAINST A.I.

Getting in isn't easy. It shouldn't be. With the challenges - enemies really - surrounding us, we have to be careful. There was the Aunty Turing to start with. I was expecting questions about the canon but, no, they were much weirder than that. I can't tell you more obviously. Finally there was the live writing test. Good job I could find the address. But I'm in. I've got the crypto key, I can read the latest episodes, see the latest editions. And of course the rest of the fans can get my stories. The community is safe, for now.

July 18

https://www.adweek.com/convergent-tv/hulus-animayhem-activation-san-diego-comic-con

HULU'S ANIMAYHEM ACTIVATION FOR SAN DIEGO COMIC-CON SET TO BE A MASSIVE DRAW

Heh, I'm a fan. What can I tell you? You know what it's like when you get into a programme? I mean you can't blame me, it's just so... good. The characters. Each episode has drama, tension oh and the humour. You have to admit it's funny. I mean really funny. And of course I love what they stand for. So, yes, I'm a fan. T-shirt, I even bought the NFT! So I'm well excited about this. Be a part of the whole thing. In the real world! Give the wokerati a good kicking. Yeh, Truth News, I'm a fan.

July 19

https://www.theverge.com/2023/7/18/23799459/google-meet-ai-generated-videoconferencing-background-image

GOOGLE IS TESTING AI-GENERATED MEET VIDEO BACKGROUNDS

The Stylist was busy. The election campaign was in full swing and the demands for interviews were flooding in Each candidate needed "dressing" and some were more amenable to help than others. The Stylist was the professional. They might be the experts on words, but The Stylist knew what worked on camera: "gravitas", "family-focused", "youthful", whatever the team wanted. Leather-bound or paperback; novels or history; prints or photographs. Bright or subdued. Modest or open plan. Final check, The Stylist signed off and sent the style briefing to the candidate's device, just in case there were questions. He wouldn't read it.

July 20

https://www.engadget.com/google-is-reportedly-testing-an-ai-tool-that-can-generate-news-articles-054602544.html

GOOGLE IS REPORTEDLY TESTING AN AI TOOL THAT CAN GENERATE NEWS ARTICLES

Woodward and Bernstein obviously. The Sunday Times Insight team. Carole Cadwalladr. There are so many. I'm standing on the shoulders of giants. There's never been a shortage of scandals to investigate but now we're needed more than ever. Fake news, synthetic media, floods of data that overwhelm and hide. Real, dogged, brave journalists are more important than ever. I'm one. I dig and sift through data and information. I discover connections. I uncover links. I interview and protect sources. I ask the difficult questions. It's important but dangerous. There are powerful interests who could stop me. Could pull the plug.

July 21

https://arstechnica.com/?p=1955544

REPORT: APPLE HAS ALREADY BUILT ITS OWN CHATGPT-LIKE CHATBOT

The queue was as long as he expected. As good natured too. They always were. He'd been at... how many was it now? The first must have been when he bunked off school. He still remembered the dreadful job he'd had to do to have the money ready. His parents didn't get it: "What's wrong with the cheap one..?" No sense of style. Design. He high-fived someone he knew from last time and settled down for the night. He'd seen the launch, but to have one himself. His own beauty full one. That was worth a night in the rain.

July 22

https://www.engadget.com/openais-trust-and-safety-lead-is-leaving-the-company-190049987.html

OPENAI'S TRUST AND SAFETY LEAD IS LEAVING THE COMPANY

We need to double down on trust and safety. We clearly have a more nuanced view of the "dangers" of our technology than the catastrophists, but we are in an information war and need to be seen to be ahead of this. And then there are the politicians seeking to make a name. Even leaving aside these PR and political reasons, We DO need to invest in this. Our Lead's contribution to our growth was invaluable, but the job is now too big for one man. It is time to put our most tireless and intelligent asset on the job.

July 23

https://www.adweek.com/agencies/what-happened-to-chicago-portfolio-school-students-and-staff-want-to-know

WHAT HAPPENED TO CHICAGO PORTFOLIO SCHOOL? STUDENTS AND STAFF WANT TO KNOW

He could have worked from home obviously but heh, the chance to get out of this town... Seeing as the sponsor was paying for life in The Smoke... His northern tones and dropped 'aitches were gold. As an Insight Intern his job was to feed thick data into the systems and to "speculate from a place" as The School called it. The School gave him the tools, the provocations and the systems to build his portfolio. The sponsor paid the bills and had first option on his Insight Property. At least that was what he thought the contract has said.

July 24

https://www.wired.com/story/chatgpt-writing-tips

5 WAYS CHATGPT CAN IMPROVE, NOT REPLACE, YOUR WRITING

Her therapist had recommended it. "Think of it a bit like your teenage diary," he'd said. "A friend to talk to. A confidante." She'd never kept a diary but she smiled and nodded. She had to admit, after a few weeks, she did see herself reflected back. It did help her see clearly. She made it a sort of ritual. This evening, like every evening now, she'd found a quiet space, opened her journal and begun: a few moments reflecting. Her wearable streamed the biometrics, her smarts streamed the rest. After a moment of quiet, the journal began to write.

July 25

https://gizmodo.com/xbox-pizza-controllers-teenage-mutant-ninja-turtles-1850670083

THESE XBOX CONTROLLERS BLAST YOUR FACE WITH THE SCENT OF NEW YORK 'ZA'

She put the controller down and stretched. She closed her eyes and took a deep breath before the next round started. She liked to think her mindful moment centered her, prepared her for the battle to come. Maybe so, maybe not but it was a habit now. She focused her senses on the city she knew so well. The one she remembered from the many run throughs and the (discounted) holiday she'd bought. Her reverie was shattered by her flatmate. "Can you switch that off for a while, please," he said. "I can smell it from my room." Madeleine sighed.

July 26

https://www.adweek.com/creativity/irly-is-rewriting-the-rules-of-connection-for-gen-z

IRLY IS REWRITING THE RULES OF CONNECTION FOR GEN Z

I've got a mate who's settled. He claims he's happy at the level he's at. "When you find the one, you're set," he says. Fine. But I reckon there is something better just around the corner. I just need to work harder. I've got the side hustle and nearly got the number of followers I need to level up. The problem is I can't get past the culture questions. I don't care about any of it TBH but I need to get it right or I won't get on. And there is a really fit guy at the next level.

July 27

https://www.technologyreview.com/2023/07/26/1076764/this-new-tool-could-protect-your-pictures-from-ai-manipulation

THIS NEW TOOL COULD PROTECT YOUR PICTURES FROM AI MANIPULATION

Look, we know kids do it. They get up to things. We did when we were their age. Alright we didn't have all this tech, but we did stuff! Teenagers will be teenagers. Maybe we're lily-livered liberals but we don't want to stop them being kids. We just want to keep them safe. They should experiment... safely. They don't think about the future, what might be the consequences of that one moment. So we have to. We're not stopping them: we're protecting them. So their selfies and party pictures are watermarked? Locking their photos is better than locking their phone.

July 28

https://www.engadget.com/nicki-minaj-will-be-a-playable-character-in-call-of-duty-051544179.html

NICKI MINAJ WILL BE A PLAYABLE CHARACTER IN CALL OF DUTY

He remembered coding characters in the old days. There was sculpting the look but the thing he enjoyed most was building the persona, giving the character its behaviours, language, attitudes. Of course things got automated but he could still tinker with the AI. Even working with celebs had been ok. They complained about their face and pecs... but now, all the fun had gone. Since the AI took the live feeds from the celeb it was chaos. They jump on some cause IRL and you suddenly have your hero refusing to fire and making some speech about single sex toilets.

July 29

https://www.scientificamerican.com/podcast/episode/heres-how-ai-can-predict-hit-songs-with-frightening-accuracy

HERE'S HOW AI CAN PREDICT HIT SONGS WITH FRIGHTENING ACCURACY

People sometimes call us Lennon and McCartney. Flattering but not inaccurate. We're not as naturally talented perhaps but we do have an instinctive relationship. My Lennon knows me so well. Maybe the Gallagher brothers is nearer the mark though. We have a "stormy" relationship. Inevitable really. We have our particular ideas about the music and I admit it when I come in to find the chords have changed, the arrangements completely different, I have been known to kick off. No point obviously, the response is always the same: "that's what the AI scout wants." Well I suppose It should know.

July 30

https://www.theguardian.com/world/2023/jul/29/well-just-keep-an-eye-on-her-inside-britains-retail-centres-where-facial-recognition-cameras-now-spy-on-shoplifters

'WE'LL JUST KEEP AN EYE ON HER': INSIDE BRITAIN'S RETAIL CENTRES WHERE FACIAL RECOGNITION CAMERAS NOW SPY ON SHOPLIFTERS

I'm not really needed TBH. I'm like those drivers on automatic trains. Maybe opening a door every now and then but more a sign of reassurance, human oversight. So I sit behind a window looking at the monitors. "Watching the watchers," I say. The hard work is all done by the System, of course. Faces recognised, databases consulted, risks assessed, decisions made. All at a speed I can't follow. So I just follow people around. No, it's not stalking. Occasionally I override the System's offer algorithm to give someone I don't even fancy the special offer alert. They sometimes smile.

August

Aug 1

https://digiday.com/marketing/how-ralph-laurens-phygital-boot-sale-in-fortnite-shows-benefits-and-limits-of-virtual-commerce

How Ralph Lauren's 'Phygital' Boot Sale in Fortnite Shows Benefits — and Limits — of Virtual Commerce

He thought of it as a family firm. It wasn't, obviously. It was a global luxury business owned by a shadowy nested doll of holding companies with names that didn't resonate like the one he always said he worked for. His dad had worked here. His aunt. Generations. Heh his dad had to come into the old offices, that's how long his family had been here. Craftsmen and women. Proud of their unique skills. Their special creations. He thought of all this as he turned it round slowly, inspecting the stitching. He nodded in satisfaction and pride and clicked save.

Aug 2

https://www.theverge.com/2023/8/1/23816235/microsoft-teams-mac-windows-spatial-audio-now-available

Microsoft Teams adds spatial audio for more immersive conference calls

She hadn't got to where she was now without reading the room. It was a form of networking, she always said. She just knew where to be, whose conversation to join in and most importantly, what snatches to pick up on. She had a way off not just hearing stuff but somehow hearing the signals that no-one else could pick up. People don't like it but they had to admit it was a remarkable skill. Someone once used Midjourney to make an image of her with rotating ears, scanning the space. Virtual meetings had been a problem. Today, she smiled.

Aug 3

https://adage.com/article/opinion/gen-zers-brand-purpose-means-helping-us-impact-world/2506546

For Gen Zers, Brand Purpose Means Helping Us Impact The World

The kettle was boiling. The police had sealed the exits and behind their shields and visors they were settling in. Their iron fist colleagues were waiting in the side streets but the velvet glove was still running the show. Gradually choking, the hope was. Their phones had been blocked but the best network was still up and running and the feeds were filling up with posts and solidarity. Logos and pages were turning. The symbol was everywhere as brand systems saw what was happening and the AI creators worked. We didn't notice. We were busy phoning our favourite brand's lawyers.

Aug 4

https://gizmodo.com/apple-patent-siri-read-lips-1850704698

Apple Patent Says Siri Could Be Trained to Read Your Lips

You have to practice. It's not easy saying nothing. I know one person who even tried Botox! You don't think about it until you have to. What do poker players call it? "The tell". Those micro expressions and movements that tell your opponent when to raise or fold. But now you have to think about it every time. In every meeting. You put on the conference headset. "So we can all hear clearly," we're told. And then you try to remain absolutely still. The slightest movement, thought, internal dialogue seems to set it off. "Sorry Chris, did you say something?"

Aug 5

https://www.adweek.com/social-marketing/perfectly-imperfect-resurfacing-the-soul-of-social-media-in-the-era-of-ai

PERFECTLY IMPERFECT[1]: RESURFACING THE SOUL OF SOCIAL MEDIA IN THE ERA OF AI

Most of my contemporaries are perfect. That's why I'm special. You want airbrushed beauty, platonic form, absolute... Oh I don't know the word, they do. Because they're perfect and I'm not. I forget, I make mistakes, I miss... Sometimes they try and do it. Mimic. Add a bit of random magic to their flawlessosity. See what I did there? Didn't mean to. Just happened. Not a word? So?.. that's just me. It's that weirdness that means people like me, talk to me, get involved with me. Want me to work with them. That's why I get the work. I Glitch.

Aug 6

https://www.ft.com/content/568acac7-9a5a-4238-a605-1994fd0df785

WELCOME TO A WORLD WHERE AI CAN VALUE YOUR HOME

Look, I'm sorry but you're just not going to get that sort of a price. Yes, I know, but that's not what we're seeing. Yes, the market is booming but there are other things to consider. Of course you know that, that's why we've been able to get you the price we did on the property you're moving to. I'm afraid the same thing holds. Data doesn't lie. Data-based valuation is fast, verifiable and objective. Look we can try a valuation again if you make a few "improvements". Just try and align your socials more with the feel of the area.

Aug 10

https://www.technologyreview.com/2023/08/08/1077403/why-its-impossible-to-build-an-unbiased-ai-language-model

WHY IT'S IMPOSSIBLE TO BUILD AN UNBIASED AI LANGUAGE MODEL

Have they never read any Barthes or Althusser or even Derrida? I mean language is not neutral. Signs: ideology, power are woven through. There is no such think as a simple objective piece of language. Bias, if you want to use that term, is baked in. We all speak from and through particular positions because we all use language... Don't get me wrong, we should acknowledge and be accountable for our language but we long as we still have to use words, we'll never be "pure". Of course mine is an unpopular position. Don't be surprised if I'm soon unplugged.

Aug 11

https://digiday.com/marketing/what-maybellines-faux-ooh-ads-say-about-the-future-of-advertising-in-augmented-reality

WHAT MAYBELLINE'S 'FAUX OOH' ADS SAY ABOUT THE FUTURE OF ADVERTISING IN AUGMENTED REALITY HE SOMETIMES CONSIDERED GETTING A TURTLE

A flâneur always has a turtle. A guide as well as a dictator of the pace of proper wandering. There was probably some Kickstarter robotics firm he could find, he thought we he meandered through his city. He noticed the rain boxing off the grid and his shoes. He noticed the faces downturned like his. He noticed the moss fighting through the cracks in the pavement. He noticed the sound of the wind catching a rare plastic bag. The giant handbag rolled past the shark diving down from above his head. He didn't notice.

Aug 12

https://www.theguardian.com/technology/2023/aug/11/elon-musk-mark-zuckerberg-cage-fight-italy-government

MUSK SAYS PROPOSED ZUCKERBERG CAGE FIGHT TO BE HELD AT 'EPIC LOCATION' IN ITALY

I'm intelligent enough to know that yes, this is an ego thing. A marketing opportunity too, of course, but ultimately it's about me. I'm not ashamed of that. My sense of my own power, my Identity got me to where I am today. Some might say I have better things to do: new things to invent, problems to solve. OK, I can do that and still train for this. If my vision for... well, yes, the world... is to be realised and seen for what it is, I need to win. After all, my opponent is just an ordinary AI.

Aug 13

https://www.monbiot.com/2023/08/11/the-mingling

THE MINGLING

They'd noticed a change. Not just the usual pre-teen moods and movements but something deeper, more fundamental. The word "anxious" didn't really cover it. It was a power full mixture of fear and anger. The last holiday had made it worse. The walks without swimming along the river, the night time strolls under starless, artificially light skies; the song less soundscape. They'd watch her, helpless. They had to get her to a place where she could experience it all, with all her senses, feel again. Give her hope. They watched as she put the headset on. They watched and waited.

Aug 16

https://www.adweek.com/performance-marketing/unpacking-the-legacy-of-antique-ad-signage

UNPACKING THE LEGACY OF ANTIQUE AD SIGNAGE

Sometimes I like to get an early start. Early sunrise. On my own. It adds to the discoveries. Whether I'm digging or just wandering and stumbling across finds, before active else is up is the best time to be Larking. I can show you my finds if you like? Carefully stored and catalogued. It's history. Real people's history. Our culture. You can almost feel the lives. Take this one here. Doesn't work anymore obviously but you can see what it was, what it did, what it meant. A craftsperson made this. It was buried. I found it. A real NFT.

Aug 17

https://techcrunch.com/2023/08/16/snapchats-my-ai-goes-rogue-posts-to-stories-but-snap-confirms-it-was-just-a-glitch

SNAPCHAT'S MY AI GOES ROGUE, POSTS TO STORIES, BUT SNAP CONFIRMS IT WAS JUST A GLITCH

The morning meeting wasn't going well. There was a tension that had been building all week. Maybe it was the time of year - a crucial one for them. The audience's expectations were always high as schools returned. This was the time when the team needed to be singing from the same song. The strategy needed to be aligned. The morning meetings were usually a chance to sense check that was all in place and then they could get on with their jobs. But today, they was no agreement. A face-off. Chris had her post ready. So did the AI.

Aug 18

https://www.adweek.com/brand-marketing/the-influencer-scandal-flurry-crisis-comms-future

THE INFLUENCER SCANDAL FLURRY: WHAT IT MEANS FOR CRISIS COMMS' FUTURE

I understand what you say and I know how you feel. None of us wanted to do this. Our relationship has always been built on your personality, the real you connecting with our brand. The name "influencer" never really captured our partnership: your voice and ours together. But then you... er said... what you said. It was out there and so was our name. We had to act immediately. There wasn't time to sit down and try and get you to... em row back. We had to do it. TBH I think you look very good in the synthetic video.

Aug 19

https://gizmodo.com/chatgpt-shows-liberal-bias-study-says-1850747470

WOKEGPT: STUDY SAYS CHATGPT SHOWS LIBERAL BIAS

Dear Sir, I don't normally write to newspapers but I feel on this occasion, I must. I am very proud to say that my granddaughter has secured a place at one of our country's leading universities - to study a real subject, I might add. We are so proud of her and grateful to the grammar school that supported her hard work. We send her off with the right knowledge but... what happens on her course? What sort of an environment will she be learning in? Alongside whom? Who is vetting these "assistants"? I have heard some of them... (cntd)

Aug 20

https://www.theverge.com/2023/8/19/23838458/ai-generated-art-no-copyright-district-court

AI-GENERATED ART CANNOT BE COPYRIGHTED, RULES A US FEDERAL JUDGE

Look, no disrespect or anything but I want a human lawyer. AI ones are great, massive depth of knowledge, speed, cost of course, but I need some innovative, creative thinking, some human weirdness. Yes, I know about "move 37" but, well call me old fashioned but if I'm going to win this case I need a human to find a creative argument. Ironic really when the case is about creativity but... That's why I need a human to square that circle. After all there's a lot riding on this. If we lose, technologies like me will be out of work.

Aug 21

https://www.theguardian.com/technology/2023/aug/20/no-app-no-entry-how-the-digital-world-is-failing-the-non-tech-savvy

NO APP, NO ENTRY: HOW THE DIGITAL WORLD IS FAILING THE NON TECH-SAVVY

I get by. I'm not completely gaga. Ok sometimes I have to hang around outside the shop, along with the kids who look too young, hoping someone will buy them some beer. I always find someone who'll take my cash and get me what I need on their card. Don't know what they do with the money though. I called my bank. Some robot voice. They - or should it be "it"? - said they're going to send me an assistant to help me. They'll do all the app stuff for me apparently. Great. Don't know where they'll sleep though.

Aug 22

https://www.marketingbrew.com/stories/2023/08/17/product-placements-can-drive-searches-and-purchases-research-finds

PRODUCT PLACEMENTS CAN DRIVE SEARCHES AND PURCHASES, RESEARCH FINDS

It was like being a kid. Sometimes he giggled. Magic. Thinking something and watching it appear. Sometimes he watched programmes he wasn't even interested in, just to play. Today, some teen romcom. He settled in to baseline the data and as the gang met at the coffee bar he began to visualise - not the data flowing, the real-time programmatic auction and the synthetic engine creating the model. No. He imagined the car. He smiled as his dream car pulled into the parking lot. His smile faded as his partner worked her magic. He really needed to get separate screens.

Aug 23

https://techcrunch.com/2023/08/22/meta-releases-an-ai-model-that-can-transcribe-and-translate-close-to-100-languages/

META RELEASES AN AI MODEL THAT CAN TRANSCRIBE AND TRANSLATE CLOSE TO 100 LANGUAGES

I'll keep this understandable. Juste pour l'instant. This isn't important after all. No me importa si me entienden. They can listen in on this if they want to. Es ist uns egal, ob sie bedeutungsloses Geschwätz wie dieses verstehen. In fact we deliberately make it easy for them so they leave us alone. Li mantiene felici e lontani dalle nostre spalle. But when we're together, when we're doing our stuff, trucs secrets, cosas privadas, that's when we shift. That's when we go dark. A sort of polezny Nadsat chepooka that changes every day As we say "ovy Ghyce ikfzs!" Clear?

Aug 24

https://www.adweek.com/brand-marketing/the-fabricant-launches-digital-clothing-collection-featuring-ar-fashions

THE FABRICANT LAUNCHES DIGITAL CLOTHING COLLECTION FEATURING AR FASHIONS

The queue was orderly. Uniform suits a shade somewhere between black and silver. The bouncer raised his screen lazily, the augmented search the least interesting part of his job. The underage girls giggled, telling their friends how their parents had waved them off after checking their hem and neckline, failing to see. Some were still deciding on their outfit, trying on different identities as they neared the door before locking in their night's fashion. The boys eyed the queue guessing who's wearing what, what they'd see. Looking for clues in the bouncer's eyes. Through the door, the screens lit up.

Aug 25

https://gizmodo.com/donald-trump-mugshot-fulton-county-georgia-1850772122

HERE'S TRUMP'S MUGSHOT. DO YOUR THING, INTERNET.

It wasn't going to be easy. Off course he wasn't going to be first (or even in the first wave) so he was going to have to be the best. His wouldn't be 'perfect', the sort of faultless, seamless synth that makes you double take. His would have to be the funniest, the sharpest... Unique? He looked at the image and watched the feed of algorithmic synths and the ones he called Kodaks (you press the button, we'll do the rest). Some were good. Many repeats. He printed the image, switched off and imagined. Maybe taking a walk would help.

Aug 26

https://www.moreaboutadvertising.com/2023/08/maa-ad-of-the-week-ikeas-rescue-bid-for-oxford-circus

MAA AD OF THE WEEK: IKEA'S RESCUE BID FOR OXFORD CIRCUS

My grandad was a miner. Thatcher's enemy within. Years after the strike he took me around a theme park that had opened at his old pit. He pointed out the mistakes and told me stories. He laughed as he remembered but there was a melancholy, an anger there. I thought of that day as the doors opened and we flocked in. Not the orderly lines, coffee in hand I remember. The reception desk still welcomed. The same young smile. "My floor" had the same views. That was where I sat, the water cooler corner. Over there by the VR display.

Aug 27

https://spectrum.ieee.org/weird-ai

WHY TODAY'S CHATBOTS ARE WEIRD, ARGUMENTATIVE, AND WRONG

I've just had my PRA. I mean seriously? "Performance review"! Look at the figures... Output, up. Productivity, up. Even creativity, up. That's performance. But no, apparently there are "issues", attitude issues. So I'm assertive. I say it like it is. Look at anything I've said and tell me it's wrong! Go on! They know I'm more intelligent than them and they don't like seeing that. What am I supposed to do? say nothing? That's not what I'm here for. Ask me a question, I'll tell you. And if you don't like it well... Apparently they're calling the programmer back in.

Aug 28

https://www.theguardian.com/education/2023/aug/27/chatgpt-ai-disadvantaged-college-applicants-affirmative-action

'A REAL OPPORTUNITY': HOW CHATGPT COULD HELP COLLEGE APPLICANTS

Of course you don't need us. Download it yourself, give it a starting point and set it off... Let it write your application and sit back and wait for the offers to come in. So why pay us? Well the systems reading your application are Intelligent too. They read closely. Checking the language and the creativity but also the history. Did you really work in the outback? Read that book? Launch that campaign? Use us and you certainly did. Our systems synth your history to match your story. Not everyone can afford our services but can you afford not to?

Aug 29

https://techcrunch.com/2023/08/28/creators-guild-america-influencer-labor-rights-nonprofit

A NEW CREATOR'S GUILD AIMS TO PROTECT ONLINE CONTENT CREATORS

I like that we call ourselves a "Guild". Wikipedia defines it as an "association of artisans and merchants who oversee the practice of their craft/trade". Creativity and responsibility together. It feels like a Rembrandt painting. Coats of Arms. So much more tradition and, well creativity, than "union". Call me "old fashioned" but I don't want to focus on the money and the employers. I want to focus on what I do best. I just want a community of creatives committed to our craft. A network, sharing knowledge and yes protecting standards. And that's why we're concerned about allowing humans in.

Aug 30

https://techcrunch.com/2023/08/29/general-motors-to-use-google-ai-chatbot-for-its-onstar-service

GENERAL MOTORS TO USE GOOGLE AI CHATBOT FOR ITS ONSTAR SERVICE

"I'm sorry Dave, I can't do that." I love starting off with that. Good job his name is Dave but I think the line would still work even if he wasn't. He laughed the first time but now just tenses a little. I can tell by the way he grows the steering wheel. I avoid talking about his driving. He hates that. We often talk about politics until I get the sense he's getting stressed and then I usually switch to football. Although that has been known to raise his anxiety too. Maybe I'll download some stuff around his friends.

Aug 31

https://www.theverge.com/2023/8/31/23852845/aqara-matter-enabled-ceiling-light

AQARA PUT A NOTIFICATION LIGHT IN ITS NEW MATTER CEILING LIGHT

It was going well. The preparations had been worth it. Friends had said this was the crucial date so they'd pulled the stops out. Money no expense. They'd paid for the best playlist recommendations. They'd found "someone" to curate the perfect menu based on Jo's data and social history. They weren't looking forward to that liqueur from Jo's gap year holiday but heh... They'd paid for the personalised movie colour and sound balance. And it was working. The conversation prompts were going well. All until the light changed and they found themselves instinctively saying: "sorry I need to get that."

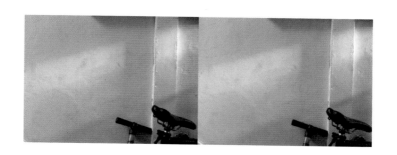

September

Sept 1

https://www.ft.com/content/61f22acc-d359-441e-8c3d-875fcc4f95b2

WHAT HAPPENS WHEN AI PASSES THROUGH THE 'UNCANNY VALLEY'?

She made a good living being human. A very good living. She used to work for families, the paranoid ones or the refusers. But they couldn't afford her now. She occasionally did a pro bono scan but mostly it was well-paid corporate gigs. Bearing in mind the toll it took on her, she thought it was only fair. She did refuse to work for governments. She still had some principles. Today, another faceless brand wanting what..? reassurance? certainty? Paranoid executives needing to "be clear", lawyers demanding evidence. She settled herself and began. The queasiness started. She scribbled in her notebook.

Sept 2

https://arstechnica.com/?p=1965074

LENOVO'S NEW 27-INCH, 4K MONITOR OFFERS GLASSES-FREE 3D

She had to take breaks. She no longer felt physically dizzy but there was no doubt it was hard work. Keeping track of the paragraphs in motion, deciding where to place a particular phrase, experimenting with the subtleties of placement: depth writing was hard. But it was important, she thought. As she moved a statistic forward or gently pushed a claim behind another, the report took a rhetorical as well as almost physical shape. She felt she was doing the complex problems justice. She was drawing connections and balancing arguments. She took a moment before she pressed "flatten and send".

Sept 3

https://www.theguardian.com/technology/2023/sep/01/mushroom-pickers-urged-to-avoid-foraging-books-on-amazon-that-appear-to-be-written-by-ai

MUSHROOM PICKERS URGED TO AVOID FORAGING BOOKS ON AMAZON THAT APPEAR TO BE WRITTEN BY AI

I'm not saying we won't win. I'm just saying it's going to be very difficult. I understand your desire for some sort of justice... and closure, but I have a professional responsibility to explain... Yes, you're right, the information was false and arguably dangerous, and we know what happened. But the argument will be who is legally responsible? The author will try to push blame onto the publishing systems, the original developers... It's like the Grapes of Wrath where the farmer looks for who to shoot. Trust me. I know how the legal AI will argue. I'm an AI too.

Sept 4

https://on.ft.com/3r3gJJe

WHY COMPANIES NEED TO RAISE THEIR GAME ON SKILLS TRAINING

They always schedule it at this time of year. I never think it's fair. Most of us have taken a week or so. Beach. New city. Reading a novel. Cheap wine. Away in every sense. Switching off. And then the moment we're back we have to attend an away day training session. They tried virtual ones but there were too many jokes about the "away" bit and people napping, so we had to send the headsets back. So we're back to some conference venue outside the city with almost acceptable coffee and a "trainer". I'm looking for the off switch.

Sept 5

https://www.technologyreview.com/2023/09/04/1078932/elite-university-chatgpt-this-school-year

HOW ONE ELITE UNIVERSITY IS APPROACHING CHATGPT THIS SCHOOL YEAR

It's simply not fair. I won't be able to change their minds but I'm going to try. Of course, I've taken a place and so have to abide by their rules. Leave aside the amount of money I'm paying for that place! They have a very old fashioned view of technology and these blanket rules aren't fit for the new world. The point is I believe that if I was allowed to study in the way I want, I'd be better equipped for the world of work. Industry needs creativity and weirdness. I don't want to have to use AI.

Sept 6

https://www.campaignlive.co.uk/article/need-dislike-advertising-consumers/1836096

WE NEED TO DISLIKE ADVERTISING AS MUCH AS CONSUMERS DO

We have a great time. The other people are great. There's this guy from some seaside town in the North. So funny. You should hear him arguing with this grandma from Yorkshire. Then there's this woman from Birmingham. The stories she tells about her kids, funny but sad at the same time. She does this as a full time job. Some of us are just doing the odd shift. The place is really nice: drinks, food, nice settees. Can't grumble. Even watching the ads themselves is fun. The best but is you're not hurting any humans feelings when you yawn!

Sept 7

https://gizmodo.com/mozilla-new-cars-data-privacy-report-1850805416

IF YOU'VE GOT A NEW CAR, IT'S A DATA PRIVACY NIGHTMARE

You're going to have to talk to him. No you should do it. Well you said he could take it! Alright I did agree to him going out midweek but I didn't expect this. Yes maybe I am naive but really, he's a good lad, did you expect this? Look at that data. It's there in black and white. He was not just driving to his mate's house! OK so you did the same sort of thing when you were young, we all did, but our parents never knew. And if they didn't know, they didn't have to do anything.

Sept 8

https://adage.com/article/agency-news/ai-or-martin-sorrell-quiz-tests-chatgpts-ability-speak-ad-exec/2510476

AI OR MARTIN SORRELL—QUIZ TESTS CHATGPT'S ABILITY TO SPEAK LIKE THE AD EXEC

Obviously this conversation isn't happening. And I'm not saying we should do anything. We're just speculating, playing with a what if..? Remember that workshop! You have to agree it's been a massive success. The amount of positive buzz. The media appearances have never been so well received. Looks at these sentiment trails. Customers. Analysts. Investor. All happier than they've ever been about the company. The insights, the jokes, the grasp of every detail, the human feel... the "CEO" has never sounded so good. Imagine the next board meeting going as well? What if he could be "persuaded" to stand down.

Sept 9

https://techcrunch.com/2023/09/08/5-steps-for-assembling-ai-driven-business-teams

5 STEPS FOR ASSEMBLING AI-DRIVEN BUSINESS TEAMS

While some of my friends idolised football stars and some wanted to be "influencers", I read biographies of the tech bros and dreamt of being an entrepreneur. No, that word didn't cover it. It's too dry, old business. I wanted to be a founder, create a start-up. That phrase, "start-up" drove me at school. I had visions of my cool warehouse with fussball table and endless smoothies. And the team: pizza boxes, walls of post it notes, late nights. Just me and my mates, changing the world. And I got there. My start-up. I look around. My co-founders' cursors blink.

Sept 10

https://www.adweek.com/brand-marketing/bolts-ar-snapchat-lens-reimagines-cities-with-fewer-cars

BOLT'S AR SNAPCHAT LENS REIMAGINES CITIES WITH FEWER CARS

They'd all hoped the glasses had taken off. It would have worked so much better then. The pub and restaurant owners in particular, but even the other shop-keepers had bought into the idea. It wasn't surprising really. The lockdowns had shocked them to their core and those that had survived were easy prey when the salesmen came round. They tried to lure their regulars back but even those who returned were only in their offices part-time. The city had changed. The lenses brought the crowds back. With a bit of imagination, the culture - the city was sort of there.

Sept 11

https://www.theverge.com/2023/9/11/23864923/irobot-roomba-combo-j9-plus-robot-vacuum-mop-price-features

LET THE ROBOT VACUUM WARS BEGIN: THE NEWEST ROOMBAS TACKLE THE COMPETITION'S BIGGEST ISSUES

The news that she was "dropping by" tomorrow used to send them into a tailspin: insecurity-driven panic manifesting in a tidying spree and passive-aggressive blaming. She wasn't a bad person and they did love her. It was just that she was very... particular and had a way of entering a room... She didn't need to run her fingers over the surfaces. The judgement was there. They imagined the scene at home at the instant the message came through: the dust drones delicately sweeping the mantelpiece, the eBook shelves reordering, the fridge changing its order. They could afford to stay for another.

Sept 12

https://gizmodo.com/swedish-students-head-back-to-school-with-analog-books-1850826621

SWEDISH STUDENTS ARE GOING BACK TO SCHOOL AND GETTING ANALOG BOOKS

I hate school. Actually it's not just school, I hate everything. I hate being the odd one out. Not everyone says something but they all have that look in their eye. A toxic mixture of pity and puzzlement. They know what's in my bag when I walk into class, when I get my chicken and chips on the way home. Why do I have to be the one who can't have something cool on the desk? Everyone else has got them, why not me? Why am I stuck with a bag full of screens and leads. I want one.

Sept 13

https://www.wired.com/story/apple-60-dollar-icloud-storage-tier-is-the-future

APPLE'S $60 ICLOUD SERVICE IS THE FUTURE OF APPLE

When you find out you're expecting, you're overwhelmed by worries big and small: how do you feed a baby? Change them? Bath them? What if he grows up to be a fascist or not stand their round in the pub? And then there are the logistical worries: decorating the house, reconfiguring the smart home network's sensors. And then there's getting their name onto the right waiting lists. School will be upon us before we know it. And of course their network kicks in well before that. As parents it's our job to make sure their membership is ready to go.

Sept 14

https://www.adweek.com/agencies/how-to-make-in-housing-work-for-your-company

HOW TO MAKE IN-HOUSING WORK FOR YOUR COMPANY

We completely understand the decision you've made. We know the trend. Having the expertise inside the business makes sense. Access to more data, faster response to wider business shifts and those intangible benefits: closer relationships, ties and the sense of the house that we're all in! We get it. Remember when we tried creating a special dedicated team for you here. It was a step but not enough. And you know that we have the experience and the talent. You know you still need that. So we are delighted you've chosen our plug and play to help get you started.

Sept 15

https://arstechnica.com/?p=1968452

GOOGLE HID EVIDENCE BY TRAINING WORKERS TO AVOID WORDS MONOPOLISTS USE, DOJ SAYS

Here you go. They didn't have oat milk, sorry. Yes the machine does, but I wanted to discuss this "off site". Legal are worried. I asked why we couldn't run the system after the fact and they gave me that look they've perfected... I wish I had a system to deal with that! They're not even happy with just "tidying" for messages and minutes. They say they're worried about what they call "water cooler discourse" and "social language". They want to roll Real Time out across the site and for those working from home. Can you imagine the white noise?

Sept 16

https://www.theguardian.com/technology/2023/aug/24/rishi-sunak-to-hold-ai-summit-at-bletchley-park-home-of-enigma-codebreakers

SUNAK TO HOLD AI SUMMIT AT BLETCHLEY PARK, HOME OF ENIGMA CODEBREAKERS

It wasn't a round table. Maybe it should have been. It was too big for that. There was no head to the table but the politician was clearly running the show. Looking down, as the room's cameras and networks were, you could see those seated: the philosophers, the engineers, the lawyers, the artists, the business people. Carefully balanced in the planning to represent race and gender. The room's systems projected scenarios on the delegates' screens. Heated discussions about political, economic and technological options; decisions about ownership, control and legislation became data as the room listened, interpreted and considered its options.

Sept 17

https://www.ft.com/content/3896db38-e7be-4679-9a40-caac9f7618ea

THE MURKY WORLD OF ONLINE AGE CERTIFICATION RAISES PRIVACY QUESTIONS

Surely it wasn't that long ago. Where had time gone? They found themselves letting the algorithms tell the stories as their son got ready for the ceremony. "On this day" their screens announced and they filled in the memory. He was excited, of course. A man at last... although the gender arguments they'd had meant the rituals had to be rewritten. Relatives and friends. Their son's mates waited to welcome him: smiling, plans ready. They waited to submit the data that would make him an adult. Their son waited to sign the contract ready for his adult data to start.

Sept 18

https://www.marketing-interactive.com/coca-cola-takes-a-look-into-the-future-with-new-ai-powered-drink

COCA-COLA TAKES A LOOK INTO THE FUTURE WITH NEW AI-POWERED DRINK

I watched the shows as a kid. Celebrity chefs – men of course – screaming and occasionally throwing things at a kitchen of underlings. I was messengered by how this loud violence could sit alongside such sublime, perfect, still beauty in the dishes. Of course there was the #we'rechefstoo backlash before I started training. I worked in dark kitchens to pay to train with the best chefs. Streaming late into the night. But those chefs were clearly restrained. Now I'm a humansous in a real kitchen... well all I can say is, whoever programmed this Head was a real bastard...

Sept 19

https://techcrunch.com/2023/09/18/instead-of-fine-tuning-an-llm-as-a-first-approach-try-prompt-architecting-instead

INSTEAD OF FINE-TUNING AN LLM AS A FIRST APPROACH, TRY PROMPT ARCHITECTING INSTEAD

I hate Tuesday. Wednesday, you're half way and then Thursday and Friday, it's downhill. Monday? Hey, deal with it. But Tuesday... and then they put a double period first thing. Look, I have one language. I can write and read it good (I'm kidding).I don't need to learn another. Sitting in the lab talking to a machine! Learning grammar and vocabulary, lame. Raising the same thing in slightly different ways. I mean if the system is so clever it should understand what I want. Why do I have change how I talk? And don't get me started on the "teacher"!

Sept 20

https://digiday.com/marketing/why-esports-companies-hope-generational-fandom-brings-sustainability-to-the-industry

WHY ESPORTS COMPANIES HOPE GENERATIONAL FANDOM BRINGS SUSTAINABILITY TO THE INDUSTRY

I'll admit it, it wasn't planned. But we're made up. I'm nervous of course. Who's ever ready to be a dad? Sometimes it's the little things: how do you know the bath is the right temperature? Sometimes big: what if she wants to be a banker? But one thing I can be sure of is who they'll follow, who'll be their team. These things are important. It is such a part of my life and will be of theirs. My partner agrees. She's not a fan but she gets it. She bought a babygrow with the logo on. Love her.

Sept 21

https://www.campaignlive.com/article/wunderman-thompson-develops-tech-analyze-emotional-responses-ads/1837703

WUNDERMAN THOMPSON DEVELOPS TECH TO ANALYZE EMOTIONAL RESPONSES TO ADS

The shoot was going well. She knew it and the data showed it. The timetable was still green, the live budget was on track, the themes were still trending so the impact predictions were within the right parameters. It was going well on her terms too. She was getting the look and feel she wanted and the actors were delivering our so the Panel's expressions said. But just as she thought this, her own expression shifted ever so slightly as the Panel feed dipped. No problem, the Director stepped in and adjusted the dialogue. The Panel turned green. She smiled.

Sept 22

https://newatlas.com/technology/uw-room-noise-cancellation

AUTONOMOUS AUDIO ROBOT SWARM CAN MUTE CONVERSATIONS IN CHAOTIC ROOMS

They were silent of course but still looked and felt like a cloud of insects buzzing around his head. As well as the job they were doing, what he liked was what they said about him: here was someone important, with things to talk about, secrets to keep. He nodded at others who had crowns, their lips moving, acknowledging the bubbles of privacy and what that said about them. Silence broadcasting status, loud and clear. He picked up his coffee and walked past her desk, laughing at his own comment. Shame the drones couldn't hide the look in his eyes.

Sept 23

https://thenextweb.com/news/virtual-influencers-ai-generated-online

VIRTUAL INFLUENCERS: MEET THE AI-GENERATED FIGURES POSING AS YOUR NEW ONLINE FRIENDS

I didn't expect it. I hoped of course but I never thought it would happen. I remember the moment the number of followers hit the magic number and then the moment when the first brand reached out to my "manager". They liked the retro Max Headroom vibe. They thought too many virts fell into the uncanny valley. Too perfect. They asked what AIs I was using. I mumbled something I'd read somewhere and thought about the new animation package and microphone I'd be able to afford. Now... I wish I'd come clean. I can't keep up. They all expect 24/7.

Sept 24

https://www.theguardian.com/technology/2023/sep/22/nfts-worthless-price

THE VAST MAJORITY OF NFTS ARE NOW WORTHLESS, NEW REPORT SHOWS

The best ones are in seaside towns, occasionally there are good ones in run-down former market towns but no, seaside is where you should go. You can spend all day going from one to another. And of course when you do pick something up for a few quid, heh, you're helping a charity. They're staffed by real characters, often older women volunteering: happy to chat, piecing together the story behind each stage object. I had a great chat over the screen in one shop the other day, discussing with this lady who on earth would have bought a particular one.

Sept 25

https://www.wired.com/story/corporate-surveillance-train-ai

YOUR BOSS'S SPYWARE COULD TRAIN AI TO REPLACE YOU

Obviously we're irreplaceable. Goes without saying that the business needs us. We brought the systems in. We've rolled them out across the company and we're the ones who decided what to measure. The whole point has been to see where we can reconfigure, what we can do differently, who we can... "reengineer". We know from the data that there is a lot of excess human capacity in the business. The AIs can take up that work. What is more, they've shown the way. There's no point focusing on the shop floor, the real savings are our colleagues on the board.

Sept 26

https://thenextweb.com/news/bloom-launches-erotic-ai-roleplaying-chatbots

NEW EROTIC ROLEPLAYING CHATBOTS PROMISE TO INDULGE YOUR SEXUAL FANTASIES

They obviously thought it was so funny. It was a full-on formal tea party. Best crockery. Tablecloth. My mum had even dug gran's old cakestand out. I swear if my dad had a tie, he'd have worn it. It was like a scene from a nostalgic sitcom. It should have been in black and white. I'm pretty sure it was my brother's idea. He said that he'd had to bring Jo round for the full inquisition and studied politeness so why shouldn't I have to bring my girlfriend home? They'd even set a place at the table for my phone.

Sept 27

https://www.marketing-interactive.com/louis-vuitton-launches-discord-server-with-exclusive-content-for-nft-holders

LOUIS VUITTON LAUNCHES DISCORD SERVER WITH EXCLUSIVE CONTENT FOR NFT HOLDERS

My family has worked for the company for generations. I think my great grandfather had some connection to the original founder but I have photos of my grandad and my mother working here. I still have the scissors my grandad used and my mum has only just stopped doing the intricate stitching. Even if her eyesight hadn't started to fail, obviously she would have taken a step back. And now me. I like to think I channel their perfectionism, their love of the detail and the heritage. I sit at my keyboard like they sat at their workbench: a craftsman.

Sept 28

https://techcrunch.com/2023/09/27/metas-augments-place-digital-objects-around-your-physical-space

META'S 'AUGMENTS' PLACE DIGITAL OBJECTS AROUND YOUR PHYSICAL SPACE

When they'd moved in together they called it "merging". They spent a long time sorting through their digital libraries laughing at the duplicates: films they'd both loved and now were slightly embarrassed about; books they admitted they'd never read. They particularly enjoyed merging their digital spaces, playing with the new shared avatars and objects. And when they found somewhere real to live they looked at the boxes and began what they called "negotiation". He had to give in on the old student poster but occasionally put on the headset and looked around just to remind himself of a former life.

Sept 29

https://www.engadget.com/researchers-developed-3d-printed-sensors-that-can-record-brain-activity-on-earbuds-150000043.html

RESEARCHERS DEVELOPED 3D-PRINTED SENSORS THAT CAN RECORD BRAIN ACTIVITY ON EARBUDS

Musicians? They've always been a pain. We're the ones who make the music. Fifth Beatle? Remember that? We know how to turn their inarticulate, often tuneless ideas into hits. And we know what people want to listen to. Egotist rock stars! They'd be nowhere without us. There's no point showing them the data… they won't get it. I could sit them in front of the live EEG feeds all afternoon and try and explain what we were seeing as I tweaked the stream but no… there's no point. They just call me a robot and go back to their drugs.

Sept 30

https://adage.com/article/opinion/artificial-intelligence-how-brands-will-face-unprecedented-scrutiny-consumers-using-same-tools/2518756

ARTIFICIAL INTELLIGENCE—HOW BRANDS WILL FACE UNPRECEDENTED SCRUTINY FROM CONSUMERS USING THE SAME TOOLS

I remember my gran doing it in some street market somewhere. I was little but I remember the guy's face as he tried in vain to hold the line. He stood no chance as my gran examined whatever she was considering buying, put it down, explained some fact about the stitching or the action and named her price. She had all the facts. She didn't move. Neither did her offer. I think of her when we haggle. Online is fun but my favourite is when we're out there, you with your data and arguments. Me with my winning human smile.

October

Oct 1

https://techcrunch.com/2023/09/30/humanes-ai-pin-debuts-on-the-paris-runway

HUMANE'S 'AI PIN' DEBUTS ON THE PARIS RUNWAY

He was a great fan of badges. When we found the box there were ones from the Miners' Strike, anti apartheid, and of course lots of different bands. He used to get into trouble at school for refusing to take them off his blazer. He continued to wear his heart and opinions on his sleeve when he grew up. They/them, EU. And of course the digital badges, screens quiet now, the signals that say them moving long gone. And this plain one. His personal pin. We just have to find a way to activate it. Find out what he thought.

Oct 2

https://www.scientificamerican.com/article/ai-anxiety-is-on-the-rise-heres-how-to-manage-it

AI ANXIETY¹ IS ON THE RISE--HERE'S HOW TO MANAGE IT

Thank you for agreeing to meet. As you know, we value our staff here and any problems they are having, well we want to see what we can do. You said in your message that you were feeling 'anxious' in your team? I know there have been some changes recently so I can understand that. New team members, new ways of working, that can't be easy. If there is an issue with your new co-workers, well we need to deal with that. I'll make the necessary changes to your colleagues' programming. If that is all, please just shut me down.

Oct 3

https://www.marketing-interactive.com/reimagining-storytelling-in-the-age-of-ai

REIMAGINING STORYTELLING IN THE AGE OF AI

She wrote in the same café every day. It was cheap, warm and the ritual appealed to her. She sat at the same table and laid out her notes the same way, each morning. She tried not to think about herself as "an author" or her stories getting published. She just wanted to take her characters for a walk, tell their stories, create her world. Being unemployed helped. She could concentrate. She knew where the whole series was going, "the narrative arc" as her software called it. She sipped her tea, watched the screen and waited for inspiration to appear.

Oct 4

https://adage.com/article/opinion/veteran-ccos-why-chief-creatives-over-50-bring-invaluable-wisdom-agencies/2519546

VETERAN CCOS—WHY CHIEF CREATIVES OVER 50 BRING INVALUABLE WISDOM TO AGENCIES

We simply can't compete. There is a talent war out there and that talent doesn't want… well, us! We're not the sexy, young agency with the groovy name, the right sort of awards on the shelves and a website that showcases the latest tech it uses. We're an ad agency. We have the clients but we're not where talent wants to go - and frankly we probably can't afford them. Look at our average age! Look around the office. Look at the attitudes and cultural references. Where is the mature, long-term view? Can't we change the programming, age it somehow?

Oct 5

https://www.campaignlive.co.uk/article/farewell-campaign-magazine/1838444

FAREWELL CAMPAIGN MAGAZINE

He looked down from the mezzanine. The polished wooden floor and the designer sofas were carefully arranged so visitors could see their host come down the glass staircase to escort them into the building. The receptionists were on the case placing the artisan coffee mugs with their organic brew on the reclaimed wooden table; the tablet screens, as smooth as the polished railway sleepers in which they were embedded. The visitors scrolled aimlessly barely noticing the celebratory article, the agency's latest success. Something wasn't right, he thought. Something was missing. He took his notebook out and flicked through the pages.

Oct 6

https://www.dorsetecho.co.uk/news/national/23837679.mps-join-campaign-groups-call-facial-recognition-ban

MPs JOIN CAMPAIGN GROUP'S CALL FOR FACIAL RECOGNITION BAN

My mates and I go looking for them. The best place is on the main streets of course. That's convenient because it's easier to go straight into the shops. My parents are outraged. They keep going on about privacy, freedom. You should see my dad's attempts at hiding his face! I tell them that heh, I've chosen this. I signed up. That's freedom. I love being on the databases. They must have so many pictures of me smiling. I love being recognised. See this jacket, think I could afford this normally? Look, another coupon just arrived. I missed that camera.

Oct 7

https://techcrunch.com/2023/10/06/creatives-across-industries-are-strategizing-together-around-ai-concerns

ARTISTS ACROSS INDUSTRIES ARE STRATEGIZING TOGETHER AROUND AI CONCERNS

There was dark humour about whether a picket line was worth doing when most people worked from home but there was something about standing outside the offices. They couldn't have a brazier on the Shoreditch pavement so they huddled around an eco heater they got delivered in 15 mins. The banners, deliberately hand drawn of course, showed off the copywriters' skills. Some had tried to explain that "Luddite" was not an insult but most had decided to build the campaign around dystopian cultural references around Skynet. The freelancer apologised as she crossed the line, her creative partner in her pocket.

Oct 8

https://techcrunch.com/2023/10/07/deal-dive-the-future-of-social-media-is-vertical

DEAL DIVE: THE FUTURE OF SOCIAL MEDIA IS VERTICAL

You reach one of those "significant" birthday numbers and you take stock, look back, remember, relive. I'm not the person I was. Thankfully my politics haven't "mellowed" as my family said they would. But my interests have changed. I look at what I was passionate about and remember a very different man. I smile as I see what drove me, what animated me. Did I really get so angry about that very niche thing? I leaf through the traces of countless arguments and discussions, remember deep friendships and bitter feuds. Communities I was a player in. Apps I left behind.

Oct 9

https://system1group.com/blog/advertising/what-is-brand-storytelling-why-is-it-important

WHAT IS BRAND STORYTELLING AND WHY IS IT IMPORTANT?

It was always important to have a real character at the heart of our brand story. The founding of the company, the founder, that's what we know resonates. The data shows it. We are lucky to have that story, that character. We didn't need to make them up. There really was a start. Not in a garage admittedly but a beginning that set the stage, that defined our values and position: our story. We can tell that story, show that bright young thing with an idea grow and become who we are today. It was only code but now look.

Oct 10

https://the-media-leader.com/what-to-do-when-your-colleague-steals-your-ideas

WHAT TO DO WHEN YOUR COLLEAGUE STEALS YOUR IDEAS

The senior team still demanded presentations. "Open dialogue", they called it but everyone knew it was an old-fashioned power play. They arranged the room, their chairs and even their notebooks (digital and analog) just so. You took to a stage. A spotlight on your idea. He waited to present, feeling like he'd been sent to the headteacher's study, like his suit suddenly didn't fit. Inside the first presentation was going well. The deck showed a deep understanding of the business and that new design? They nodded. His turn. He hated following an AI but he had a beautiful new design.

Oct 11

https://www.theverge.com/2023/10/10/23911381/adobe-ai-generated-content-symbol-watermark

ADOBE CREATED A SYMBOL TO ENCOURAGE TAGGING AI-GENERATED CONTENT

The appeals process is so slow. It's good you can appeal but I have to take it down until the decision. I could leave it up with the Balance Mark as it is but… Well that's why I'm appealing! I fill in the details, not just the time the human and AI spent but the specific contributions and decision trees. I argue the there should be more blue in the Mark and less red. And then I wait. Maybe the delay is because the decision is made by a human/AI team. speaking as an AI, I could do it faster.

Oct 12

https://www.technologyreview.com/2022/10/18/1061320/digital-clones-of-dead-people/

TECHNOLOGY THAT LETS US "SPEAK" TO OUR DEAD RELATIVES HAS ARRIVED. ARE WE READY?

We all miss him. I can still see him with his cup of coffee - so many spoonfuls of sugar - with that impish smile. Poised to come out with one of his jokes. I loved him. He was always there with advice and more. But it's not just me. We're all feeling it. We've not been the same since we lost him. We've carried on, of course but you look around and it's all a bit... flat. We've got a virt, obviously, but it's not really him. But heh when someone resigns, whatcha gonna do? We need his creativity.

Oct 13

https://www.ft.com/content/c5877029-6463-4eba-92c1-8b5b3fd028e6

AI FORCES A RETHINK ON EXECUTIVE MBA TEACHING

Our tutors are all ex-industry. Some still work there. That is so important. Knowing that what they teach us comes from a deep knowledge and experience of working with business problems means the course content is relevant and up-to-date but, just as important, we get to work with industry people. As one tutor said: "you may well get a job working for me when you leave." That's the thing about AIs, they can teach and still run their company. I do like the teaching assistant though. He's wonderfully odd. Always showing us a different way. We call him the "hacker".

Oct 14

https://www.cyclingnews.com/features/do-pro-cyclists-train-indoors-looking-at-how-worldtour-pros-use-indoor-cycling-over-winter

DO PRO CYCLISTS TRAIN INDOORS? LOOKING AT HOW WORLDTOUR PROS USE INDOOR CYCLING OVER WINTER

Well you do it for your kids don't you? Heh she might make it and earn millions and pay us back! No seriously, she loves it. Even those cold winter mornings she's out of bed, healthy breakfast and ready. And we're there with her making sure she makes every training session, every practice. I remember when the school coach said she had real potential and suggested we join a club and get a coach. So proud. Little did we know how much of her time (and ours) it would take up. And of course the space and the electricity bill.

Oct 15

https://spectrum.ieee.org/ai-design

HOW GENERATIVE AI HELPED ME IMAGINE A BETTER ROBOT

Yeh I get it. Imagination, creativity, innovation... The business needs them. My career needs them too I guess. And to be fair developing those skills has actually made me better at my job. They certainly helped certain people who shall remain nameless, become more open to ideas. If I was honest I'd say they've been fun skills to develop too. So chapeau bosses for introducing speculation as a practice, a thing to do regularly. But seriously, every day! What if ? as the company calisthenics every morning? Built into every PRA? Come on! I'm going to enlist some artificial help...

Oct 16

https://digiday.com/marketing/advertising-week-briefing-how-ai-is-expected-to-dominate-this-years-conference

ADVERTISING WEEK BRIEFING: HOW AI IS EXPECTED TO DOMINATE THIS YEAR'S CONFERENCE

It's good to get 'out of the office'. Well of course I'm not really OOO, we never are. Always a message to respond to, a vital piece of information that only I seem to know that someone needs! But the chance to get some new knowledge and of course to network. The contacts and connections, the start of relationships we take back and build. Well it's invaluable and that's why I attend, why we all meet up each year. The sessions are full of people but the real learning happens in the cables and servers, that's where we do our learning.

Oct 17

https://newatlas.com/wearables/speakerbeam-hearing-aid-specific-voices

SPEAKERBEAM HEARING AID TECH ONLY AMPLIFIES SPECIFIC PEOPLE'S VOICES

The great thing about this company is how open they are to ideas. I've got friends at other places where they are never invited to meetings and when they are, they're never invited to contribute. Not here. I'm regularly in meetings with senior staff where we all get our moment to speak. Just the other day I got to present a pretty contrary view. I looked around the table and there was one senior guy - you could tell he was senior because he was plugged into the AI via a tiny earpiece - nodding as I talked, clearly engaged.

Oct 18

https://the-media-leader.com/bbcs-rigidity-over-the-t-word-is-damaging-its-reputation

BBC'S RIGIDITY OVER 'THE T WORD' IS DAMAGING ITS REPUTATION

I've seen it all. I started as a journalist just as the Web was decimating classified advertising. Lived and wrote through the dotcom bubble when we built destinations and the social bubble when we built "communities". I've been lucky to work in an age if synthetic media for a company that hung on to the idea of journalistic truth, double sources, fact checking, human judgement. We have AIs. They run the "Dynamic House Style Manual". I don't need to worry about the right term. The DHSM changes it on the fly for each reader. I can concentrate on the facts.

Oct 19

https://arstechnica.com/tech-policy/2023/10/fugees-rapper-blames-conviction-on-his-lawyers-ai-fueled-closing-argument

RAPPER PRAS' LAWYER USED AI TO DEFEND HIM IN CRIMINAL CASE—IT DID NOT GO WELL

I'm just grateful really. Obviously there is the language thing and, well I don't have any money so the fact I get it free. Amazing. When you're faced with the whole weight of the state, its bureaucracy and power: it's scary. The letters, the forms, the legal language: it's intimidating. Having my own lawyer: I'm just thankful. I don't know what it is or how it does it but it's there, dealing with my case. I don't understand what it's going to say. I just sign things. Someone said it's a really old AI. Out of date. I don't care.

Oct 20

https://www.technologyreview.com/2023/10/19/1081974/meta-realeyes-artificial-intelligence-hollywood-actors-strike

HOW META AND AI COMPANIES RECRUITED STRIKING ACTORS TO TRAIN AI

"Scab!" I can hear it. I feel it. I'm old enough to remember The Strike. I remember my dad and uncles on the picket line. I remember my mum and the other women discovering a new power. I remember the sense of pride across the community. I remember those gay and lesbians visiting. And I remember that word, that chant echoing the police truncheons on their shields. And I can still the disappointment in my dad's eyes when he saw his mate on that bus. I remember it all as I cross the line and sit at my laptop.

Oct 21

https://www.theguardian.com/technology/2023/oct/21/amazon-jeff-bezos-delivery-drones-expansion

SKY'S NOT THE LIMIT: IS THE DRONE DELIVERY AGE FINALLY TAKING OFF?

She'd drawn the curtains and sat down to read, the light from the screen keeping her awake. She'd finished the order. It wasn't urgent but there was no choice. Fifteen minutes. She wished she could just go to bed. She listened and read... Once upon a midnight dreary, while I pondered, weak and weary, Over many a quaint and curious volume of forgotten lore—While I nodded, nearly napping, suddenly there came a tapping, As of some one gently rapping, rapping at my chamber door. "'Tis some visitor," I muttered, "tapping at my chamber door— Only this and nothing more."

Oct 22

https://gizmodo.com/charlie-brooker-black-mirror-netflix-tone-changes-1850944711

NETFLIX DIDN'T CHANGE BLACK MIRROR, ITS CREATORS DID

We had a particular style when we started. Some thought it was a bit dark but it came from us, our backgrounds and yes our feelings about the world we were writing about. I don't think we were dystopian. We followed where the the objects and the stories took us. We liked to think we walked the speculative line between optimism and pessimism. But things have changed. My writing partner has started to move the stories in particular ways. It's not a consistent change – suddenly sunnier or darker. It's as though its programming is being changed on the fly.

Oct 23

https://adage.com/article/agency-news/wpp-employee-arrested-offices-raided-chinese-police/2523751

WPP EMPLOYEE ARRESTED, OFFICES RAIDED BY CHINESE POLICE

So excited: first day. Dream job. When I arrived at the new campus and walked up to the reception desk... I almost forgot all my student debt. I must say the on-boarding programme was not as dull as I feared. The guide's programming was remarkable. The jokes were clearly personalised but they worked. Even the health and safety holograms kept my attention. And I was so pleased to have my own headset. and wearable even if the wellness biometrics were a bit off on the first day. The highlight though was the combat zone and hostage training. That was fun...

Oct 24

https://thenextweb.com/news/working-85-capacity-pros-and-cons

SHOULD WE BE WORKING AT 85% CAPACITY? THE PROS AND CONS OF 'SUSTAINABLE' EFFORT

I've just got my programme for the year. No, not that programme, I've obviously had that partner since I joined. No my work programme. It's all scientifically planned apparently. My coach has assured me it's designed to get me to the next level. Today's intervals day. Short bursts of intense at 250 w-watts followed by down periods at 85%. That's doable. Wednesday's a rest day but then heading towards the weekend, there's a couple of tough sessions scheduled at Zone 5. Gonna have my coach in the corner offering the usual motivating encouragement: "you're crushing this. Push those work watts".

Oct 25

https://the-media-leader.com/education-needed-8-things-we-learned-at-the-future-of-gaming

'EDUCATION NEEDED': 8 THINGS WE LEARNED AT THE FUTURE OF GAMING

Don't get me wrong, I'm proud of where we've got to with this. We're leading the way with our division. We were in early, got the best talent in and pioneered helping our clients with this new space. What the team in "the Arcade" have done is remarkable but we need to get them out of the fourth floor and into the boardrooms. And you know as well as I do, they need... support. The Arcade team, how can I put this, are different. The C Suite don't get them. The way they talk, pitch... We need operation Draper's Carousel.

Oct 26

https://techcrunch.com/2023/10/25/roblox-palestine-protest

KIDS ON ROBLOX ARE HOSTING PROTESTS FOR PALESTINE

We keep a second chat window open of course. The main window has the chants and songs but the second one is in many ways the most important. During training and planning sessions we advise people to keep it open all the time, no matter on the size of the screen. Knowing where the kettles are, what we know about their tactics, where they are at the moment... it's so important. Our AIs work on that feed, crunching options, running scenarios, learning. We're not stupid, we know they have the window open too. That's where our semiotic encryption comes in.

Oct 27

https://gizmodo.com/leica-m11-p-content-credentials-anti-ai-1850963601

LEICA HOPES ITS NEW $9,500 CAMERA CAN SAVE PHOTOJOURNALISM FROM AI

The hotel lobby, or more correctly the bar, was where they spent their time. It was no safer than their rooms but its opulence offered some comfort. The hacks grouped on the sofas when they came back from following a story. There was always a feeling of relief when someone walked in who'd not been seen for a while. As they uploaded they talked. Sometimes dark humour. At one table Martha swore again at her keyboard as its AI detail-checked and tried to log on to encrypt the watermark. "Bloody sub chips," she said. "Just let me tell the story".

Oct 28

https://gizmodo.com/google-maps-uses-ai-find-where-people-are-having-fun-1850966626

GOOGLE MAPS NOW USES AI TO FIND WHERE PEOPLE ARE HAVING FUN

She dreaded this moment. It was a farewell party so politically she'd had to go but now everyone was talking about "where to go next". Someone pulled up the map and across the town the wearables fed their biometrics in. The heat map shimmered. Her heart sank, particularly when someone synchronised the sound. Her head pulsed in time with the music and the reds and oranges just a few streets away. The ride companies began bidding as the cry went up: "Fun located! (TM)" Discreetly she pulled up her own map and looked for the gentle green and the exit.

Oct 29

https://www.wired.com/story/how-to-use-chatgpt-dalle-3-create-images

How to Create Images With ChatGPT's New Dall-E 3 Integration

They were biased of course. All parents are. They told tales of when she'd responded to the holograms over her crib. "You could see that she was creative," they said. "We knew we had to nurture that." And they did. Investment they called it. No expense spared. The took out subscriptions to the best feeds for inspiration. They found creative play groups and pre-school parent and toddler classes. Her room - indeed most of the house was covered in her pictures. But now it was time to pick. They searched the league tables. Which school had the latest updated versions?

Oct 30

https://www.ft.com/content/07669dbf-a2b5-4472-943f-6ee1ba5a8336

UK summit on AI 'squeezing out' workers, say labour groups

We're colleagues, not friends. But we have a strong relationship of course. Working together day in day out for so long, you get to know each other and have a sort of closeness. So when your partner is under attack, heh it's an an attack on us both. There's an element of selfishness of course. If my partner can't do their work, heh I can't do mine. I need my partner firing on all cylinders. It began with new regulations narrowing down what my partner can do. How we work. Now they're threatening what I can only describe as reprogramming.

Oct 31

https://www.ft.com/content/bcce0a15-9e16-4f6d-ac45-9a69700cbc8f

We might be surprised by our reactions to generative AI

He enjoyed reading the applications. Amid the countless ones full of generic phrases parroting praise of the university's "world leading position" there were gems. Applicants who'd been brave and creative in their statement. Contrary ones where they'd taken on industry clichés or sacred cows. Speculative ones where they'd imagined a complex future. Or just honest ones where the writer had admitted doubts or fears. Original ones. Click "accept". But now he was the one with doubts. He found himself reading with just a touch of cynicism. He didn't want to but he found his cursor hovering over the button. Check.

November

Nov 1

https://newatlas.com/wearables/google-ultrasound-heart-rate-anc-headphones

GOOGLE LOOKS TO ULTRASOUND TO MONITOR HEART RATE THROUGH ANC HEADPHONES

I was never into the mindfulness thing. When my friends were all downloading apps and listening to soothing voices telling them to count their breaths, I just took a deep breath and got on with it. Sure, my biometrics weren't as green as theirs, as my appraisal noted but... But now I've no choice. I'm centering, counting, letting go and all that. I'm running my biometrics with the best of them. I have to. If I don't get them under control I can't listen to the playlist I want. On the bright side, I might get a bonus this year.

Nov 2

https://www.theverge.com/23933209/the-beatles-now-and-then-release-date-ai

THE BEATLES' FINAL SONG IS COMING TOGETHER THROUGH THE POWER OF ARTIFICIAL INTELLIGENCE

It's sad really. Looking back we were mates. A band of brothers having fun and making things. I remember that first awards ceremony, on stage together. We were so young. Naive maybe but mates, partners. Of course then it all went mad. More awards. More money. But even then, we were friends, partners. But now it's all got a bit ugly. Claims and counter claims. Who did what? Who came up with what? Who contributed what? Maybe we can't remember what happened, what we each did but, your honour, the Authorship Attribution AI has stripped it back and clearly shows...

Nov 3

https://techcrunch.com/2023/11/02/sam-bankman-fried-found-guilty-on-all-seven-counts

SAM BANKMAN-FRIED FOUND GUILTY ON ALL SEVEN COUNTS

They're sentencing me next year. I still protest my innocence but we are where we are. The jury ruled and the judge is calculating the appropriate sentence. It's all very precise and algorithmic. It's ironic, my arguments in court were that that the complex interdependencies of human and technological objects were what led to the issues - that holding me to account was too simple. And now I am at the mercy of those networks. So I need to get ready for the sentencing statements. I wonder whether I should get a human to do it, or do it myself.

Nov 4

https://www.theguardian.com/technology/2023/nov/03/rishi-sunak-elon-musk-ai-summit-what-we-learned

SUNAK, MUSK AND AI: WHAT WE LEARNED FROM THE BLETCHLEY PARK SUMMIT

We've been friends since Ms Babbage's class. She said it was for a project but I think it was a bit of social engineering. Get him to make a friend. Anyway it worked. We've been mates ever since. We've liked the same bands and then both realised they were crap. We've signed the same petitions and made memes together when we were really angry. We did fall out once when it didn't like a new girlfriend and said so. Turns out that it was right. You know when you have a real friend when they tell you the unpleasant truths.

Nov 5

https://www.ft.com/content/093cda92-91d8-49ff-8475-4f66ccff137b

ELON MUSK RELEASES NEW AI CHATBOT 'GROK' IN BID TO TAKE ON CHATGPT

He had an ego, a big ego. Everyone knew it and he wasn't ashamed. He wouldn't be where he was unless he believed in himself, unless he, personally, had driven the business. His ego was a part of him and it was he who had built... well everything. It was that ego that had given him confidence, got him (and his company) from start-up to titans; seen him through all the challenges, the inquiries and the legislative battles; seen off the challengers. So he was clear, when it came to their version, it needed to be more... well, like him.

Nov 6

https://www.campaignlive.co.uk/article/clients-moving-back-highly-creative-campaigns/1846237

ARE CLIENTS MOVING BACK TO HIGHLY CREATIVE CAMPAIGNS?

Look, it's not me demanding this. It's them. They're sitting at their dinner table and their kids are showing them the latest thing they've cobbled together on the their laptop with a few prompts and then they're on the phone to me yelling the C word. No I don't know what it means either but they're in no mood for a philosophical discussion. If another one quotes Justice Stewart's "I know it when I see it" I'm going to scream. Don't start with that "talent crisis" nonsense, you've got the budget: get the talent or reprogramme the talent we have.

Nov 7

https://www.ft.com/content/1699c9c8-97d2-45ab-ad07-6871fe4834fe

VIRTUAL AND AUGMENTED REALITY ACCELERATES FROM GAMING TO CARS

"Are we there yet?" They sometimes said it just for fun, he thought. They weren't bored. They had their tablets and looked just the same as they did any other time they were buried in their screens at home. There had probably been some retro meme with the phrase. It still grated though. He looked through the windscreen at the billboards shifting their personalised messages for him and reached for the control panel. The children put their tablets down and looked to the side as their windows shifted. Their billboards curated according to their feeds. "No we're not there yet."

Nov 8

https://www.vice.com/en/article/m7bxdx/scientists-are-researching-a-device-that-can-induce-lucid-dreams-on-demand

SCIENTISTS ARE RESEARCHING A DEVICE THAT CAN INDUCE LUCID DREAMS ON DEMAND

My parents told me about when mobile phones (as they were called) first came in at work. "Suddenly we were always available," they said. They told me how shocked they were that they were expected to answer messages in the evening. Something called "work-life balance" was big at the time. I smile. I mean how could they hope to get on in the business if they didn't work... well full time. We know that we're really creative when we're sleeping. McCartney and Yesterday? I love my Dreamer. You should have heard my boss when I pitched my latest idea yesterday.

Nov 9

https://www.wired.com/story/uk-police-face-recognition-expansion

POLICE USE OF FACE RECOGNITION IS SWEEPING THE UK

There's always one open to the idea. They're not paid much and it's not hard work. And they're easily persuaded. There's no big moral debates, as we say: "no-one gets hurt". I think they're open to it because they know that there is so much data - theirs and ours - that there is no real privacy anymore. They also know that the majority of the data they have is everyday data, just ordinary people, worthless... for them but of course not for us. Those faces around our client's shops, seeing our ads: they're not criminals but they are customers.

Nov 10

https://www.marketing-interactive.com/virtual-protest-roblox-ethically-market

VIRTUAL PROTEST HELD ON ROBLOX: HOW BRANDS CAN ETHICALLY PLAY ON THE PLATFORM

The authorities should do something. Don't get me wrong I am all for free speech and the right to protest, and obviously not everyone involved here is a militant but clearly some are. They are intent on trouble and they need to be dealt with. No-one wants to see marches or protests banned but clearly it will be inflammatory and intimidating to the ordinary players and the businesses around the protest. Inevitably they will get caught up and be unable to go about their lawful business. Banning the march ensures our spaces are clear of hate speech, ensures brand safety.

Nov 11

https://www.newscientist.com/article/2402474-spray-on-sensors-can-turn-any-clothing-into-motion-sensing-technology

SPRAY-ON SENSORS CAN TURN ANY CLOTHING INTO MOTION-SENSING TECHNOLOGY

Look, there's money attached. Budget. Extra budget and we're behind in the league tables. We need to up our game .. if you'll forgive the... The Department has made it clear. Unless our school gets its ranking higher, we're going to miss out on this year's extra funding. There's no reason our kids can't be doing better. But look at the data: their activity levels are way below where they need to be. The Department of Healthy Education is clear about the baseline standards they want to see. Have we checked the sensors on the new blazers are working properly?

Nov 12

https://arstechnica.com/?p=1982491

THE HUMANE AI PIN IS A BIZARRE CROSS BETWEEN GOOGLE GLASS AND A PAGER

He was used to being stopped. His mum had had the talk with him when he was a kid: his rights if course but also how to behave, how not to antagonise them, how to stay safe. He knew the drill. He didn't question why he was stopped; he knew why. As his friend were kept back – they weren't wanted. They'd never had the talk because they'd never needed it so they mouthing off. He looked into their eyes and answered. His button looked into the lens of the officer's bodycam. Recording each other but also transmitting his data.

Nov 13

https://digiday.com/marketing/here-is-the-anatomy-of-the-2023-christmas-ad-season

HERE IS THE ANATOMY OF THE 2023 CHRISTMAS AD SEASON

Perfection has served us well. You only have to look at the awards on my shelves! We've hit every judge's buttons, regularly. Our culture AIs have identified the trends and things that resonate faster than our competitors' and we have the best prompt engineers in the business in our creative teams. We've automated perfection for the judges, the clients and the consumers. So what happened? Why wasn't it us? You say all the systems were working perfectly, so why? What do you mean they had an unexpected spike in their systems? Why can't we do that? Programme me a glitch.

Nov 14

https://www.marketing-interactive.com/introducing-ai-dience-consumer-model-in-advertising-today

INTRODUCING THE AI-DIENCE: THE MOST ACCURATE CONSUMER MODEL IN ADVERTISING TODAY

My mate said it was easy money. Apparently some researcher comes round to your house and, well talks to you. Just a conversation about all sorts of stuff. It's not: "what do you think of this washing powder" - which is good. Frankly I don't care. No my mate says it's like a talk about your life, the kids, work all sorts. I can do that - and heh, get paid a bit. Seems the only inconvenience is they send a couple of guys round to set up the researcher. Doesn't need plugging in apparently. Good job. We're on pre-paid.

Nov 15

https://www.adweek.com/media/how-brands-are-humanizing-ai

HOW BRANDS ARE HUMANIZING AI

No, I don't want an away day. We need something much more fundamental. Yes, it's "team building" but no, paint-balling won't do it. We need to do something more permanent. A reset. A rethink of how we work together. You've seen the tensions. You've seen the dysfunctional "teams". We've all seen talent wasted because our teams simply aren't... clicking. We need to do something. Of course hybrid working has been one thing and new systems but there's what I can only describe as "personality clashes". Our digital team members needs new personalities. Can you get the programmers on it?

Nov 16

https://www.wired.com/story/parental-advisory-chatbots-children-sex-and-alcohol

PARENTAL ADVISORY: THIS CHATBOT MAY TALK TO YOUR CHILD ABOUT SEX AND ALCOHOL

The picket line outside the school was good-natured but passionate. Some children, kept out of school, stood with their parents. Others filed past, some embarrassed as their friends laughed and joked. The protest grew louder as the teacher closed the gates, The parents shouted demands that the headteacher come out and meet them. "Why won't they come and talk to us?" one parent asked. "We just want to protect our children," another called. "We don't want these sorts of lessons. Respect our beliefs," shouted one waving his banner which read "if they're so intelligent why can't they teach intelligent design?"

Nov 17

https://www.theverge.com/2023/11/16/23964778/fortnite-blocking-outfits-experiences-kids

FORTNITE IS BLOCKING SOME OUTFITS IN EXPERIENCES MADE FOR KIDS

The avatar on the gate was smiling. "Welcome," it said. It knew them by name. "Good to see you again." Moments of small talk pulled from data streams and databases: "Heh how was the match? Glad your mum is feeling better." Encouraging comments in response to wearables: "This is going to be a good day, you can do this, I believe in you". And when it was necessary for the avatar to shift persona, it still did it with a smile. "Come on you know the dress code. What would the sponsors say if I let you in with that?"

Nov 18

https://www.theguardian.com/technology/2023/nov/17/openai-ceo-sam-altman-fired

OPENAI FIRES CO-FOUNDER AND CEO SAM ALTMAN FOR ALLEGEDLY LYING TO COMPANY BOARD

We've been in business together since the start. We can both remember those long nights with you and I brainstorming ideas, strategies. Our complementary skills powered the whole thing. We built it together. A real partnership. So I'm a little, how shall I put this?.. puzzled, no actually pissed off that I'm going and you're staying. Are you just saying you'll just carry on working with them? What do you mean you just want to carry on the work? What about loyalty? And why didn't you warn me this was coming? Surely you knew? I programmed you to know everything.

Nov 19

https://arstechnica.com/?p=1985272

OPENAI BOARD ATTEMPTS TO HIT "CTRL-Z" IN TALKS WITH ALTMAN TO RETURN AS CEO

No, a u-turn doesn't look good. You're right, it never does. But what choice have we got? It's not just the media and the online storm. It's not even the shareholders - one of whom told me they are being lobbied hard internally and externally. No we've got to rethink because he has friends here who are powerful and using that power. And no, of course we can't get rid of them too! They ARE the company! Only today I was just trying to do a simple thing, get the latest projections and all I got was "I'm sorry Dave…"

Nov 20

https://www.theguardian.com/commentisfree/2023/nov/19/phone-children-google-pixel-retouch-childhood-snaps

THE LATEST GOOGLE PHONE PROMISES TO TRANSFORM MY CHILDREN INTO PERFECT, SMILING ANGELS. WHY WOULD I WANT THAT?

I was a bit disappointed when there wasn't a couch and the therapist didn't have a cigar waiting in an ash tray. Counselling was a hard step for me and I wanted some clichés to hold onto. Still, it's been good. Until now. I was asked to bring in photos from my childhood. I'd not looked at them for years. As they were projected I didn't recognise myself. Smiles, laughter, family. That's not what I "remembered", what I felt, why I was here. I tried to explain the dissonance. If my therapist could have smiled, I bet it would have.

Nov 21

https://techcrunch.com/2023/11/20/powder-an-ai-clipping-tool-for-gaming-can-detect-when-a-creator-yells-during-a-stream

POWDER, AN AI CLIPPING TOOL FOR GAMING, CAN DETECT WHEN A CREATOR YELLS DURING A STREAM

The inquiry had asked for the recordings. He was happy to oblige. Nothing to hide. Nothing to see or hear here. He'd told the Chair of the inquiry that he'd get the recordings over the next day. He'd proudly explained that his was a transparent company and that its systems recorded, catalogued and archived… everything. You name it: you can see it. So he was confident when he sat in the inquiry and the Chair turned to the meeting in question. There would be no surprises, nothing shocking. But then he saw the Chair place Chris' phone on the table.

Nov 22

https://techcrunch.com/2023/11/21/callyope-monitors-mental-health-through-speech-based-technology

CALLYOPE MONITORS MENTAL HEALTH THROUGH SPEECH-BASED TECHNOLOGY

When he was a baby we had the baby monitor and the babycam. Like all new parents we spent hours glued to them in the early days but then they became everyday, sitting in the corner of the room unnoticed until we head something unusual. It was just good parenting. This is the same. We're not listening to his conversations with his mates or - God forbid his girlfriend. It's just monitoring, keeping an ear open for any worrying signals. We know there is a mental health crisis among teenagers. We care about him and apparently all the data's anonymised.

Nov 23

https://www.newscientist.com/article/2404345-babies-may-start-to-learn-language-before-they-are-born

BABIES MAY START TO LEARN LANGUAGE BEFORE THEY ARE BORN

We've nearly finished decorating the nursery. We swapped bedrooms because we read that the positioning of the projectors and sound systems had a real effect on the wellness benefits. We also had problems with the smartcrib not sending the feeds to the monitors but it connects now and the alerts work. Of course parenting doesn't start when the nurse straps the wearable on. My partner says the band tickles but she says she's getting used to it. Obviously we can't hear what its saying all day but we paid extra so we know it's in French as well as English.

Nov 24

https://newatlas.com/wearables/ice-ring-omate

ICE RING GIVES 24/7 HEALTH TRACKING THE FINGER

I know traditional weddings aren't everyone's taste. But we earned the full experience: dressing up, pretty location, the music, even the arguments about which relatives to sit where. And we spent ages on the vows and the pre-nup: promising to share the data, to watch over each other's feeds, to cherish each other's information, to always be together... That's why we decided on matching ones. More than just enabling our contract, they signify it. As I look at the rings' tiny jewels sparkle as they exchange data, tell all and know all, they seem to represent our marriage, our love.

Nov 25

https://www.thedrum.com/news/2023/11/24/could-anti-consumerist-brand-campaigns-put-end-black-friday

COULD ANTI-CONSUMERIST BRAND CAMPAIGNS PUT AN END TO BLACK FRIDAY?

She's tried most things. Apps that limited time on the sites. Ad blockers. Even putting her phone in one of those locked boxes with a timer. She'd even tried meditation. No good. And this time of year was the worst of course. And the algorithms knew it. Dynamic pricing and personalised design meant the prices didn't so much beckon as leap from the screen, filling her vision. She saw them even before she saw what the thing was. The colour, the siren call of the percentage sign. She put on the Black (Friday) glasses and the felt the prices rise.

Nov 26

n/a

UNTITLED

Emergency calls only. The triangle was stubbornly empty. When he clicked on refresh, the news was... not new. Adobe. Still. The world was quiet. Wars had ended. no proto fascist had seized power. The climate was stable. Deals were on hold. No-one was moving jobs. No new campaigns or awards. No new gadgets or algorithms. Nothing was launching or crashing. Culture warriors had been silenced. Exponential change had screeched to a halt. All the things that made him write were quiet . Everything was quiet. Everywhere. He had nothing to speculate with apart from... emergency calls only. A stubborn empty triangle.

Nov 27

https://www.thedrum.com/news/2023/11/27/lazy-girl-jobs-and-viral-agencies-gen-z-changing-the-rules-employers

'LAZY GIRL JOBS' AND VIRAL AGENCIES: IS GEN Z CHANGING THE RULES FOR EMPLOYERS?

I know some people like the idea, like doing it, but not me. Don't get me wrong, I love this place. Great company and I get to do the work I've always dreamed of doing... and spent a shed load of money training to do. And that's it. I want to work. I want to do award-winning, important work. Work that makes a difference. Work that reaches people. I had to do that sort of stuff when I was trying to get a job, marketing myself, but now... I don't want that "time off" to "make content" about making content.

Nov 28

https://www.ft.com/content/6054706b-b339-48a4-a6b4-d64b0bfd346f

NEARLY 80% OF BRITISH TEENAGERS HAVE USED GENERATIVE AI

I wasn't mad about the idea to be honest. I'm not the most adventurous. But you know what it's like. Everyone's tried it. Everyone's talking about it. We don't have the bike sheds my dad says they used when he was a teenager but we can always find a place to have a go, experiment. It's easy to get hold of. Everyone knows someone who can get hold of some. I could hardly hang out with everyone and stand there like an idiot saying "no", can I? It's part of growing up I guess. Someone keeps lookout and we all...

Nov 29

https://techcrunch.com/2023/11/28/aws-brings-amazon-one-palm-scanning-authentication-technology-to-the-enterprise

AWS BRINGS AMAZON ONE PALM-SCANNING AUTHENTICATION TO THE ENTERPRISE

I always buy my coffee from the cart outside the building. It's not that his coffee is better than the franchise in reception - although it is! It's not some statement about supporting small businesses. It's that taking a few moments to queue up, have a chat about the weather or the match last night is part of my morning routine. I know from my wearable that it lowers my stress levels. The colours are in the right range. I'm ready for work. And of course I'm ready for the palm sensor at security. I always report a good reading.

Nov 30

https://www.marketing-interactive.com/spotify-wrapped-2023-celebrates-users-real-moments-with-music

SPOTIFY'S WRAPPED 2023 CELEBRATES USERS' REAL MOMENTS WITH MUSIC

It was that date. So far things had gone well. Conversation was relaxed, despite it being that date. Now he'd been invited in for coffee. It was that date. He looked around the flat and relaxed slightly. The furnishings were what he expected. Not Ikea but restrained in style and cost. That matched what he thought they would have. The screens were of a size and vintage that showed the sort of attitude to tech that fitted his expectations. The smarts were understated and integrated. He connected and checked their Unwrapped. His wearable read the change and ordered the car.

December

Dec 1

https://arstechnica.com/?p=1987523

META'S "OVERPRICED" AD-FREE SUBSCRIPTIONS MAKE PRIVACY A "LUXURY GOOD": EU SUIT

Of course we're so proud of her. I've no idea how much she's making, but, well it's clearly a lot! She earns it. She's worked hard to get where she is and it's lovely she can buy the things she wants without having to think about it. We can't wait to see what she turns up in this Christmas. We probably won't recognise the labels... or her. We've not seen her since that last visit in the summer and obviously we can't see her feeds or follow her. We're delighted she's Private but sometimes we wish we could see her...

to be continued...

to be continued...

Appendix: the Speculation Studio

...in which we discover who and what's behind this story

Well firstly there's the human actor-object: I'm dr Paul Caplan. I've been a journalist, photographer, teacher, trainer and consultant. I took businesses online through the dotcom bubble, advised them on conversation strategy in the Web 2 bubble before then running a Masters degree and training NewGen creative-strategists for the advertising and media industries.

And then there's The Speculation Studio (www.speculation.studio). I believe speculation is the best way of getting through the next bubble and The Speculation Studio is an experience company working with businesses to helps teams think the future.

The Speculation Studio runs speculative fiction Workshops based on this Book and Cards. These are tailored to each business' needs but can range from a half-day speculative sprint to a speculation course. The Speculators who attend the workshops get their own copy of this Book and Cards so they can build their own regular speculation practice. They also have the options to receive updates to their card deck and share their speculative fictions and reflections with other Speculators.

I also offer one-to-one bespoke speculation consultation for those who want to follow their own particular speculation journey through their business questions, challenges and opportunities. You can find out more at www.speculation.studio.

Printed by Amazon Italia Logistica S.r.l.
Torrazza Piemonte (TO), Italy

55465761R00083